DREAM

BY ZARA RAHIM
WITH ZIYAD RAHIM

"The miracle isn't that I finished. The miracle is that I had the courage to start."

John Bingham

DREAMING BIG

Siblings journey across seven continents to break six world records in marathon running

BY ZARA RAHIM
WITH ZIYAD RAHIM

© Copyright 2020 Zara Rahim & Ziyad Rahim
ISBN: 9798663341967
Imprint: Independently published

All rights reserved. No part of this book may be reproduced or transmitted in any form or by any means, electronic or mechanical, including photocopying, recording, or by any information storage and retrieval system, without permission in writing from the publisher.

DISCLAIMER

This book is written purely as an inspirational story about a marathon journey. The authors and publisher have made every effort to ensure the information in this book was correct at the time of publishing. The authors and publisher do not assume and hereby disclaim any liability to any party for any loss, damage, or disruption caused by errors or omissions, whether such errors or omissions result from negligence, accident, or any other cause.

The information in this book is not intended to replace any part of marathon or long-distance training. Like any sport, marathon and long-distance running pose some inherent risk. The authors and publisher advise readers to take full responsibility for their health and safety and know their limits. It is also always advisable to consult a medical expert before setting out on any exercise program.

FOREWORD

By Nadia Rahim

Watching your children grow takes nerves of steel. You see them when they are young, toddling towards a high slide and slowly climbing up the steps. You are in a dilemma; do you run over and help them, or do you leave them free to learn through experience? I was always the mum who took a step back and watched how each of my children reacted to whatever the situation may be. I would only run in if they were in extreme danger. My heart has been in my mouth on many occasions, watching them attempt things that I feared they might not be able to manage. However, through it all, they have invariably proven me wrong.

I had this same feeling the night the kids told us what they wanted to do. We were sitting at the dinner table when the first conversation started about breaking a world record. Both Mekaal and Zara decided to join their dad on the world record stage. As I listened to the conversation, that *heart in the mouth* feeling washed over me. Would they be safe? Would they be able to do it? I kept my doubts to myself and let them go ahead and plan their adventure. They were full of excitement and enthusiasm, something rare in children that young.

Many of our friends and family were less than excited about their proposed exploit. I understood their misgivings, but I was never one to stand in the way of my children's goals. What could I do as a parent? Support! And that's what I did. I supported them through their excitement, was there for them on the course, I held them in my arms when they were tired, and I made sure they were always safe. Their world record meant so much more than the record itself; it helped us reconnect as a family. It showed us our strengths and our weaknesses, and it completely changed our family life in such a positive way.

It also gave me time to myself and gave Ziyad a stint at solo parenting. I think that most mums would agree that we never have enough alone time. Just a little time by ourselves, time to miss our kids. Ziyad's and my parenting approaches are very different. I am very scheduled and always have something planned, whereas Ziyad prefers to go with the flow. The time they spent with their dad was always filled with incredible memories and stories that I loved hearing about when they returned from their various adventures. I also learned that kids are very resilient and surprise us with their strength. As part of their marathon training, they had to return from demanding weekend trips and jump straight back into school. You know what? They did it! No complaints, no excuses. They knew what they had to do. I am immensely proud of our whole family. We became 'Team Rahim,' and we lived the essence of what teamwork is all about.

TABLE OF CONTENTS

Introduction 10

Chapter 1 The Early Years 14

Chapter 2 Birth Of Our Running Career 21

Chapter 3 Breaking The World Record: The Plan 25

Chapter 4 Continent No. 1: Europe 36

Chapter 5 Continent No. 2: Asia (DNF) 46

Chapter 6 Continent No. 2: South America 53

Chapter 7 Continent No. 3: Antarctica 62

Chapter 8 Sightseeing In Antarctica 90

Chapter 9 Robbery In Chile And A Missed Flight To Rio 96

Chapter 10   Continent No. 4: Africa 108

Chapter 11   Continent No. 5: North America 123

Chapter 12   Hollywood And The Vomiting Episode 136

Chapter 13   Continent No. 6: Asia 146

Chapter 14   Continent No. 7: Oceania 152

Chapter 15   Official World Records 162

Chapter 16   3 Peaks Challenge 164

Chapter 17   Love Hate Relationship With Karate 176

About The Authors 181

INTRODUCTION

By Ziyad Rahim

Two years ago, our children, Zara and Mekaal, surprised us all with the application of their mental and physical tenacity to accomplish a feat that is beyond the capabilities of even most adult athletes. Completing a marathon is not easy; it requires years of preparation and much hard work. To run a marathon on all seven continents at the tender ages of 10 & 11; well, that is unheard of. Accomplishing something of this magnitude requires the mindset and resolve of a gladiator. During my seven continents, record-breaking journeys in 2013 & 2014, I was flying around the world at weekends and working in my day job on weekdays. The constant travel and time zone changes caught up with me after a while. However, with Zara and Mekaal, it never seemed to be an issue. They watched movies on the long-haul flights, completed marathons on weekends, visited amusement parks, played with penguins, and were back at school the next day as if nothing had happened.

For me, the greatest challenge was finding suitable races for them around the world. We were careful not to expose them to overly demanding events in extreme weather conditions, and we did not want them to miss school. So, the choices were limited. Moreover, due to their ages, the majority of race directors did not allow them to enter citing liability concerns. It was easier for these rigid rule-followers to simply reject their entries rather than try and find a loophole. It all began with the race in Antarctica, where the premier race organiser only allowed them to partake in a half marathon. So, I found another organisation that would accept them. There were similar issues in North America, Africa, Australia, and Europe. For every 10 to 15 rejections we received, there was always one race director who was willing to make an exception. Some of these officials knew me after my years of marathon globetrotting, while others were total strangers.

I am highly indebted to the following organisers who trusted my children's abilities and permitted them to race. Special thanks go out to the DAP team in Chile, Charlie Alewine in the USA, Billy Pearce in Australia, Eric Wright in South Africa, the British Heart Foundation in Scotland, and Abdurrehman Ghanem in Qatar for allowing the kids to participate in their events.

Following our globetrotting adventures, the book project went onto the back burner for two years. Zara and Mekaal were too young back then to fully express their feelings; hence the material was not rich enough to create a book. This year, Zara and I reviewed all our race videos and photographs, reliving our journey in the process. We discussed the book layout in detail and decided to initiate the project. Zara asked me to help her write the book, and I agreed. Thus, readers may find some words in this book are generally not part of a 14-year old's vocabulary. Those words are surely mine, or, as Zara would say, *"Dad, you are stuck in the last century."*

Over the last year, both Zara and Mekaal researched the countries and cities we visited extensively to learn more about the events in history, current affairs, and places of interest in these many varied locations. They have both developed a keen interest in topics related to climate change and its effect on global flora and fauna; and Antarctica in particular. They learned about apartheid in South Africa and completed thorough research on the history of waterways in the UK. All these wonders, among their many other observations and sentiments, are elucidated in the following chapters.

Zara and Mekaal never wanted the book to be just about marathon running and world records. Instead, they aim to take readers on a journey way beyond the certificates and accolades they received from running around the world. They want to show the world what ordinary human beings can achieve, regardless of their age, if they have the will and determination to fulfil their goals. Zara talks openly about her fears and dislikes; and how she overcame those to complete tasks that weren't in her comfort zone. The book is about the life lessons learned during the marathon quest; many of which cannot be learned in any formal school syllabus.

I hope you enjoy the book!

CHAPTER 1

THE EARLY YEARS

From a very young age, in fact, from my very earliest childhood memories, marathon running, country-hopping, and travelling around the world were three things that were business as usual in our household. Mum once mentioned to me that my expected birth date had clashed with the Mississauga Marathon in 2006, which dad had signed up for. He waited until the morning of the race in case my arrival in this world might be delayed and he could participate in the event. Luckily for him, I was stubborn and didn't want to leave the comfort of the womb. So he went ahead and completed the race while I stayed inside for another two weeks before the doctors induced mum. A year and a half later, my brother was born, and together, we formed a close bond, though he continues to annoy me a lot of the time with his typical boyish pranks.

I don't remember much about my life in Canada as we moved to Dubai after my brother was born. After barely a year in Dubai, dad was offered a new job in Qatar, and we had to move again. So, before my third birthday, we had already moved three times to three different countries. In between, we travelled a lot as a family.

Our summers were spent in Scotland, and during spring, autumn, and winter, we would jet off around the world for one or two-week holidays. By the time I was five, I had visited over 40 countries. Of course, I don't remember too many of the places we visited in those days, but I have been told that my brother and I were very easy-going travellers and never complained. Looking back at our travel photos, I vaguely remember running inside the Cu-Chi tunnels in Viet Nam, patting a tiger in Thailand, being carried in a basket up a mountain by a Sherpa in Nepal, and even being dressed up like a gladiator outside the Colosseum in Rome. All these adventures sounded incredible, especially now when I get to see all the family pictures and videos. The one thing in common about all those trips were pictures of dad running a marathon.

I always wondered how he managed to find a marathon wherever we went travelling. Maybe he was just so lucky. Later, though, I discovered that he first looks for a marathon in a new country that he is planning to visit, and then plans his trips around the race.

As a family, we have always supported him whenever he runs. I recall the time when we were up in the mountains of Nepal, and he was taking part in the Annapurna 100. It was New Year's Day, and we were shivering beside the start line at 4 am, waiting for the race to start. Mum then came up with the bright idea to trek up part of the mountain, and she hired two Sherpas to carry Mekaal and me in their straw baskets. I was fascinated while going up those steep mountains of the Annapurna range, drinking hot tea, and eating daal bhat at the local restaurants.

Since dad is a slow runner, mum always found a way to keep us entertained while he was on the course. So, most times, we would draw pictures and create banners saying "Go Daddy Go" or "Congrats Dad" and waved them to him as he approached the finish line. Even when he went abroad by himself to run a race, we would wait for him to return back home and surprise him with banners as he entered the house. So, in a nutshell, our lives revolved around running, travelling, and supporting each other.

My first ever long-distance race was a 3 km in Dubai. We flew from Doha to Dubai for the weekend when I was five years old. Dad was running the full marathon, but he signed the three of us up for the fun run as well. I remember running the full distance without stopping. Mekaal struggled as a chubby three-year-old, but he still completed the distance. It was the first race in which we all got medals. My brother and I were so happy that we both slept wearing our bling that night.

As we got older and mum started her business, our vacations became limited, and we could only travel during school holidays. Dad continued his running and would travel at weekends to a different country, run the race, and fly back on Sunday. He always brought us something wherever he went. I remember he went to Antarctica for the first time in 2012 and brought back stuffed penguins for us. Then he showed us the pictures and videos of penguins and seals. Both my brother and I absolutely adored the birds and wanted to play with them. Mekaal asked him if he could have a baby penguin as a pet, not realising that they wouldn't be able to survive the Doha heat. I remember dad promising us that he would take us both to Antarctica one day. One quality that impresses me the most about my dad is his honesty to deliver what he promises!

After 2012, my dad took his marathon passion to a new level. I think he met some crazy runner on the Antarctica trip, and upon his return, told us that he wanted to break a Guinness World Record (GWR). We were young enough to not fully understand what that meant. So, he bought the record book from the shop and showed us all the records in it. Some of the records were quite intriguing; the longest moustache, smallest bird, shortest person, heaviest man, and so on. We all thought it would be a cool idea for my dad to be in that book. A few months later, he started planning the trip and resumed his training. At night he would come into our bedroom and tell us stories of how the planning was going. We just pretended to look interested, but at that age, we could not fully comprehend most of the things he mentioned. However, one thing we were taught by our mum was to support each other, and that's what we did. I think all we were interested in back then was what daddy would bring back for us from abroad, rather than understanding about his marathons. In January 2013, he set off to Antarctica to start his GWR quest, and over the next 40 odd days, he flew all over the world on weekends and worked in the office on weekdays. We, however, got to see him at least four evenings a week and hear his stories of marathons around the globe. His final race of the challenge was at the North Pole. Around that time, we watched the movie 'Polar Express,' and we had a fair idea of what the pole would be like with elves and all the Christmas stuff. We even asked him if he would catch the polar express to get to the North Pole. When he returned after breaking the record and showed us the pictures from the pole, we were a bit disappointed that it did not look as tempting as it was in the movie.

Upon receiving his first Guinness World Record, he decided to break another one, courtesy of another 'crazy' runner whom he had met in Antarctica. Later, we found out that the runner was Dr Brent Weigner, who had broken every imaginable world record in long-distance running. A few years later, my brother and I had the privilege of running beside him at various events. So, here was my dad, again running around the world on a crazy schedule to break the record for the "fastest time to complete an ultra-marathon on each continent." It was the same routine, flying every weekend from one continent to another, working in the office during the week and, of course, more stuffed penguins for us to add to our collections! In 2015, after breaking ten Guinness World Records, I think he got a little bored and wanted to do something else. So he decided to take his passion to yet another level and started his marathon travel company to organise events that no one else in the world had thought of.

As for me, before I hit double-digits, my life was as normal as any other kid's. School in the morning followed by extracurricular activities in the afternoon, and some fun time playing with neighbours in the evening. Mum had enrolled both Mekaal and me in 'Playball,' a sports and movement program for kids where you get to learn several different sports and about teamwork in a 40-minute class. She was so impressed with the curriculum that she decided to purchase the business from the existing owner. Mum has now been successfully running it for almost nine years. My other activities included karate, swimming, and drama classes. Little did I know that a few years later, I would embark on a life-changing journey across the globe, a quest that only a select few in the world have been able to achieve in their lifetime.

CHAPTER 2

BIRTH OF OUR RUNNING CAREER

Dad had always wanted us to lead a healthy lifestyle. Back then, growing up in Qatar, there were not many opportunities for kids to take part in track and field or other athletic events. Apart from one running club, where runners would meet up for a Friday morning run and coffee, there were no organised races, even for adults. So, he came up with the idea of creating the Qatar Running Series. Simultaneously, he launched an ambitious project of organising cruise adventures through his newly-formed company, Z Adventures. That same year, we took a European cruise vacation with my family and grandparents. It was our first time on a cruise ship and Mekaal and I loved it. All-you-can-eat food all day, including a huge breakfast selection followed by burgers, pizza, and other delicious food for lunch and then a formal sit down dinner in the evening. In between meals, my brother and I were hooked on ice cream cones and unlimited splashing in the water park. After dinner, we used to go to shows or watch movies in the open-air patio. We never wanted the trip to end and wished we could make it an annual trip.

So, when dad informed us about the marathon cruise vacations that he was planning, we immediately agreed to join him. As luck would have it, the cruise adventure coincided with our one-week winter school holidays, so mum allowed us to accompany dad on the trip. There was one catch, though. If we were to go along with him, we had to run a 10 km race on each island that we would visit. With Qatar Running Series (QRS) events in full swing, we signed up for all the races to prepare ourselves for the cruise. Back when QRS began, my brother and I were the only two juniors to take part in the races. However, as the events became more popular over time, more and more kids started signing up. Now, in its fifth year, out of 350 - 400 runners who participate, 30% are juniors.

In January 2016, just after my brother turned eight, we flew to Puerto Rico from Doha. It was a long journey with transits in Madrid and Miami. There were around 40 runners from around the world on this trip. Most of them were older people, but we had a nice time with them. The funniest was Kamika Smith from Hawaii, who made lots of jokes and entertained us during and after the races.

I remember, one time, we were locked out of the room as dad had taken the key with him and was nowhere to be found. So, we picked up some doughnuts from the breakfast bar and sat outside the room, waiting for him. A few minutes later, Kamika walked past and upon finding us there, started singing:

"Poor kids, locked outside the room
Eating doughnuts, having fun."

The events on each island were tough because of the Caribbean heat. Every morning our ship would dock in a new country, and we would walk out and meet the local organisers. Dad was instrumental in setting up these events, and now I realise how hard he worked to ensure everything ran smoothly. At every island we visited, we were greeted by government officials who would organise a schedule for us. Reporters from local newspapers and TV stations came along too and interviewed the runners. Mekaal and I were also interviewed by TV channels and were featured in newspapers on some islands. We would normally finish our 10 kms early and then head back to cruise ship while some people were still running marathons.

It was indeed a great trip, and we were able to see first-hand how these crazy people travel around the world, run marathons, and have a great time. That same year, our parents enrolled us in TriClub Doha, where we started taking part in triathlons. In order to do well, we had to learn proper swimming techniques. So, we joined H20 Swim Club in Qatar Foundation to hone our skills. After a month of extensive training, we were both able to move from the bottom of the pack to podium finishers in triathlons and aquathons.

CHAPTER 3

BREAKING THE WORLD RECORD: THE PLAN

It all started as a joke over dinner one night, sometime around September 2016. My brother, fresh from winning a QRS event, boasted how fast and amazing he was and that he could easily beat my dad in a 5 km race. We all know my dad is not a fast runner, but he can run forever. So, the conversation went like this:

MEKAAL: *Dad, you are so slow that I could beat you in a 5 km by five minutes.*

DAD: *You may beat me in a 5 km, but what about a marathon?*

MEKAAL: I could beat you in a marathon, too, if I trained.

DAD: Not yet, son, you don't have the strength just yet to sustain that pace over a longer distance.

MEKAAL: I think I do. I can even break your world records.

DAD: OK, let's see if you can. Do you want to run a marathon?

MEKAAL: I want to run a marathon on all seven continents. If I do, will that be a record?

DAD: Yes, it will be, as I know of two runners, a male and a female, who set the record when they were both 12 years old.

MEKAAL: OK, Zara, let's do it together as we are both less than 12.

ME: Are you crazy! No way am I running a full marathon on all seven continents.

MEKAAL: C'mon Zara, don't be a spoilsport. We can do it. Maybe we should ask dad to give us a reward after we complete the record?

DAD: OK, done deal. You can ask for anything you like if you break the record.

MEKAAL: I want a PS4. All my friends have one, and I don't. I want to play with them.

ME: OK, in that case, I want a phone since I am the only one in my class who doesn't have a smartphone.

DAD: Deal!

That innocent-sounding, five-minute conversation over dinner set the tone for an endurance journey that would transform us from normal school kids into world-record-holding adventure-runners. I still, to this day, cannot fathom how we got ourselves into this challenge. Why did our dad agree to buy me a phone and Mekaal a PS4? We could have just asked for them as birthday presents, much like all our classmates had. Moreover, it would have been way cheaper for him to spend a thousand dollars on two gadgets than fork out maybe over 60x more money to take us around the world to break the record. I asked him about it last year, and he said that I was too young to understand the reasoning. Maybe one day, when I am older and a bit wiser, I will.

Knowing my dad, he probably stayed up longer than usual that night thinking about and planning his next project. Over the next couple of weeks, he talked about nothing but the plan. It was getting a bit irritating, and I knew mum was getting annoyed as well. But, that's my dad; once he puts his attention to something, there is no-one in the world who can make him change his mind. My brother and I did not complain too much, as we knew we really wanted the rewards at the end of it. Besides, he was planning another cruise marathon adventure four months down the road, and we wanted to remain in his good books so that we could tag along. This time, though, he had raised the stakes and wanted us to aim for a longer distance as part of the preparation. Mekaal was the first to attempt going longer as he completed his first half marathon at the age of eight in December 2016. The following month, we embarked on the same journey to Puerto Rico as the previous year for the 2nd edition of the Southern Caribbean

Challenge. We were a year older, and therefore both mentally and physically stronger. We also knew the courses and the challenges each one would throw at us. In the 2nd race in St. Thomas, US Virgin Islands, dad was pacing me in the 10 km, and I told him I wanted to attempt the half marathon. Looking at the conditions, with the hot sun baking down and very little shade along the seafront, dad refused and said it was too dangerous. I wasn't very happy as I was the last one in the family who hadn't achieved the half marathon goal. After the 10 km, he asked me to stop and return to the ship. Thinking about it now, he was right; he knew the dangers and didn't want to harm us. He had enough experience to know what was right for us.

My break came just two days later after we docked in Barbados. The course was tailor-made for me to attempt the half marathon. It was in a beautiful, small and shaded park beside the cruise terminal. With the Caribbean Sea on one side and cooling trees on the other, almost the entire course was sheltered from the hot sun. It was also the shortest of all six courses with a one-kilometre loop. Mekaal and I set off at a decent pace and enjoyed each other's company. All the other runners were giving us high fives as we passed them. Although my brother wasn't planning on completing a half, he decided to continue on, to support me. In about two and a half hours, the big moment came as my brother and I crossed the line for the 21st time to complete what I felt was the toughest thing I had ever done in my life up to that point. Finishing was a huge relief, but at the end of it, I could proudly call myself a ten-year-old half marathon finisher! I had completed what I had been asked to do by my dad. For the remaining days on that trip, I thoroughly enjoyed myself by spending a lot of time on the ship, eating ice creams, and relaxing in the pool with my brother.

When we got back to Qatar, it was business as usual for us—attending school in the mornings, doing homework in the afternoons, and pursuing extracurricular activities in the evenings. Our weekends were packed with either QRS events or TriClub triathlons and aquathlons. The running and multisport calendar in Qatar usually goes from October to May. From then on, it becomes too hot to be competing in endurance sports outdoors. For our marathon training, we did not follow any specific routine. Our parents recognised that if they had put us on a strict training regime, we would have lost interest. Instead, they focused more on us exercising for at least an hour every day with a combination of running, football, swimming, and karate.

While we continued to train and go about our daily routines, dad was busy planning the marathons for us. I could feel he was getting frustrated with the planning, and he did not fully share all the issues he was facing. A few times, I overheard him complaining to mum about various race organisers who were not keen for us to take part in their events. I assumed it was due to our age and the risks it posed for the race directors. My parents were also managing other issues. Once, I overheard mum talking on the phone with her family, justifying that it was alright for us to run a marathon and that they were responsible parents. Obviously, our relatives were concerned about our safety. I think the problem was that none of them had ever taken part in a long-distance race. So, in their eyes, any sport that involved running for a long period of time was harmful to an individual. One day, our parents decided to take us to a doctor for a check-up. We had our blood tests done, and then they privately spoke with the doctor while we sat outside in the corridor. I don't know all the details but judging from their body language on the way home, I could tell they were satisfied. The next day, I asked if everything was OK, and dad said, "*Just continue with your daily routine and have fun."* That was enough for me to realise that everything was fine.

With the school year-end approaching and the temperature in Doha rising to 50c, our outdoor training was more or less over. Just like every summer, we were getting excited about flying to Scotland to be with our cousins and also looking forward to playing outside in the park. My dad was busy, as usual, with work and also planning a seven-country marathon challenge in Africa. He wanted us to join him, but with all the travelling between the countries, mum said, "No." Travelling in the target African region involved us taking six or seven injections to protect us against yellow fever and other diseases. I hate needles, so I was glad mum decided against accompanying him on that tour.

In Scotland, it was back to fun times. We played outside from morning till evening. There were no long runs, no swimming or karate classes, and, above all, no school. We were free to do whatever we liked. I hung out with my cousins making YouTube videos; we would dance, sing, laugh, and eat. On weekends, we would head into the hills on gentle hikes and take bike rides in the country-side. It was never-ending fun, well, so we thought until one morning mum broke the dreaded news. She came into our room and said:

"So, Zara and Mekaal, I have some news for you. We will be running our first marathon next week."

"What?" I exclaimed. "Next week, where?"

"Well, it will be in Glasgow!" she said, with a big smile on her face.

"But mum, we haven't trained in a long time, and we can't run that distance," I said, feeling worried.

"Will dad join us for the race because I don't want to do it without him?" questioned Mekaal.

"Yes, he's flying over next weekend for a few days and will run with all of us," said mum.

"Oh no, I don't want to do it. I want to do it next year when I am ready," I moaned.

"OK, but if you wait till next year, you will not be able to break the world record," mum replied.

"C'mon Zara, stop being a baby. We need to break the world record, and I want my PS4!" Mekaal said in his usual deep voice.

"AARGGHH, OK whatever, let's do it. I want the phone too, as he promised me," as I reluctantly agreed with them. I was missing dad anyway, so I wanted him to come over and see us.

The moment finally arrived when dad walked out of Edinburgh Airport on a rainy summer's day in July. He was not only excited to see us, but he was very keen for us to start our marathon journey, which he had been planning for over six months. We were scared but also excited to take on the challenge. He didn't go into much detail on our forty-minute' drive back to Glasgow, but he insisted that we head straight to a sports store to pick up some essentials for the race. We stopped off at the 'Glasgow Fort,' an outdoor shopping centre, and picked up thin running gloves, waterproof trousers and jackets, hats, and an extra pair of running socks.

Over dinner that same evening, we went over the details about the race. At that point, we did not know the course, not that we cared anyway. All we were told was to get to bed early as we had to leave the house by 7 am. My grandma asked us what we would like to eat during the race and then made us nice sandwiches. I don't remember having butterflies in my stomach that night when Mekaal and I went to bed. We were actually looking forward to it. It was a new chapter in our lives, and we could not wait for it to start!

CHAPTER 4

Continent No. 1
Europe

BHF GLASGOW TO EDINBURGH TREK
Saturday 22 July 2017
Scotland, UK

Start line of the marathon in Glasgow, Scotland

I am not sure if it was a coincidence that we started our seven continents journey in Scotland, with it being my mother's country of birth, but I am glad we did, as we were very grateful for family support along the way. Born in Canada to a Pakistani father and Scottish mother, and having lived the majority of our lives in Qatar, my brother and I considered ourselves lucky to represent all four countries. So, it was really special to start the record quest in my favourite country.

Most of our cousins from my mum's side live in Glasgow, and they were thrilled to be able to cheer us on at different points along the course. We left the house at 7 am, and it took us around 30 minutes to arrive at the Glasgow Science Centre, the starting point of the race. Upon arrival, we walked into the building to collect our bibs and some merchandise. It was quite cold and windy that day, and there were lots of people beside the start line. The atmosphere, though, was lively and festive, with plenty of families in costumes and with bagpipes playing in the background.

It was an unusual race and not something that I had experienced before when we used to accompany our dad on his big-city marathons. The event was organised by the British Heart

Foundation to raise money for charity and promote a healthy lifestyle. The race was divided into three segments. The full event was a 100 km trek from Glasgow to Edinburgh, a 56 km day-trek from Glasgow to Linlithgow, and a 40 km night-trek from Linlithgow to Edinburgh. The minimum age to register for the race was 18 years. However, special permission was granted by the organisers to allow Mekaal and me to take part in the race, as long as we were accompanied by our parents, who also had to sign a waiver form. Since the marathon distance is 42.2 km, the BHF management even allowed us to start our course in Glasgow and finish it at the checkpoint at Falkirk Wheel at 43 km.

The race briefing was at 7:50 am. I did not listen to it closely and had no idea what the route would be like. I don't know if it was the cold weather or nervousness, but I did not feel too great. Nevertheless, my family was with me, and I knew they would take care of me. One unusual thing about the race was that when the guns went off, no one ran. I was so used to race starts where runners start sprinting from the second it starts. However, in this case, everyone walked slowly along with their backpacks, chatting with each other and enjoying the bagpipes. It looked and felt more like a carnival parade than a serious marathon event. There were certainly no skinny, super-fit Kenyans to be found at the start line, and no one seemed too bothered about running or setting any course records. My brother had warmed up for five minutes before the race like he usually did when competing in Qatar. He is a fast runner and always wants to be on the podium. As the race started, he looked at me and said:

"Let's go, Zara; we need to pass these slow people. They are blocking our path".

I could tell he was getting anxious as this was not what he was used to at the start of a race. My dad calmed him down and told him to just walk and enjoy the scenery. He said we could start running later when the course opened up. Both my parents were carrying backpacks, which included drinks, snacks, and extra sets of clothes, just in case. They also carried waterproofs, a mobile phone, and a first aid kit. We were both advised to take it slow as it was our first marathon. There was a generous time limit, so we could take our time and still finish the race.

As the field opened up, we started running, but that didn't last too long because we wanted to conserve our energy. The course was interesting as we trekked the small paths, crossed bridges, and walked through tunnels along the river. I remember we walked through one tunnel and mum started singing, and it echoed, which was a bit embarrassing! About half an hour into the race, we had to walk up a long stairway, which brought us to Kelvingrove Museum and Park. It was a beautiful park, and we stopped to take some pictures and admire the museum building and lush green lawns. At that point, I asked my dad how far we had come. My jaw dropped when he told us that we still had 39 km to go.

"Are you sure, dad? It feels so long!" I enquired. He just smiled, told me not to think about it, and to keep moving. From there on, we increased our pace slightly and continued our run and walk pattern. Our plan was to run one kilometre and walk the next. Pretty soon, we entered a trail that ran along the Forth and Clyde canal. The views were amazing, with the canal on our right and bushes on the left. There were many trekkers on the course, and since we were the only kids, we got loads of encouragement. At the 10 km mark, we saw the signs for the aid station. It was a welcome relief. Just about then it started to rain, so we decided to go in and relax for a while. Mum quickly produced some sandwiches from her backpack. They tasted so good and gave us

the energy that we needed. We washed them down with a few big gulps of Irn-Bru, to follow the proper Scottish tradition.

After about a fifteen-minute rest, we set out again on the course. Fresh from the break, we started running again, and pretty soon, we got into a rhythm as we passed a lot of the walkers. Both Mekaal and I felt good and relaxed until we approached the half marathon mark. One thing that scared me the most on the course were dogs. Both dad and I have a fear of dogs. He once told me that during a marathon in a Croatian suburb, he came across two big dogs sitting in the middle of the road. Instead of running past them, my dad stood there for 15 minutes and waited for the owner to come and move them.

As we continued our march forward, we got increasingly frustrated with the canal. The scenery had not changed much, and our legs were getting heavy. I could tell Mekaal was not his usual cheery self. I think all that walking was getting to him. I remember dad once mentioned that if you ask a runner to walk for a long time, he will get tired quickly. I believe this is what we were going through at that moment. There was a long period of silence, and then out of the blue, I heard this conversation between Mekaal and dad:

Mekaal: *"OK, that's it. I quit. I cannot do this anymore."*

Dad: *"Are you serious, Mekaal?"*

Mekaal: *"Yes, I hate this race. I cannot walk anymore. I am tired."*

Dad: *"Well, son, you have two options; you either walk back 21 km to the start line, or you walk forward 21 km to the finish line. The choice is yours."*

Mekaal: *"What if I stop here and ask grandma to come and pick me up?"*

Dad: *"Do you see any roads here? We are in the middle of nowhere on this path, and even if we leave you here, your grandma will never be able to find you."*

Mekaal: *"OK fine. I will continue."*

Just at this tough time, we saw my aunt and our cousins Amie and Eva running towards us. The sight of them brought a huge smile to our faces. We stopped for a little while to talk to them, took some pictures and moved forward. However, we were still walking along that canal and our patience was running thin. To keep our minds off the course, mum started a history lesson. She has a wealth of knowledge and told us that these canals were built during the industrial revolution over 200 years ago. They were used to transport goods from one place to another before the road network was built. Nowadays, their main use is recreation, as almost all the transportation of goods is done via rail and road. The two main canal systems are the Caledonian Canal in the north, which links the Atlantic Ocean with the North Sea, and the Forth & Clyde canal in the south, which linked Glasgow and Edinburgh, connecting with the Union canal. She told us the finish line was at the Falkirk Wheel, an engineering marvel. In 2002, it opened to allow boats to be carried over 79 feet to join the Union canal. Before the Falkirk Wheel was built, it took a series of 11 locks to transfer boats from one canal to the other. It was fascinating hearing about it, and we became so engrossed in the conversation that we did not even realise we had covered another 10 km. Then, suddenly, Mekaal and I heard someone shouting our names. It was our cousins Aleena and Ayana with my aunt Shaezia. They were waving to us from the top of a bridge. We were thrilled to see them as they had made posters to motivate us. We stopped at a nearby café and had ice-cream. It was a good break, but we knew we had to continue. So we said our goodbyes and continued our journey towards the Falkirk Wheel. We were running and walking, and even singing as much as we could. My dad played music on his phone to keep us entertained. One particular song I remember was Ed Sheeran's *"The A-Team."* One of the lyrics was *"Cool girl, no phone."* Dad pointed at me and started laughing. He said, *"You are that cool girl who does not have a phone!"* It was, indeed, ironic, and we all laughed together.

We marched on, and soon the sign markers told us we were 3 km from the finish line. Then the heavens opened up again. I had never experienced torrential rain in Scotland; it was literally bouncing off the ground, and our shoes filled with water. We were exhausted, and our legs were stiff. However, just when we felt we could not take it any longer, we had our first glimpse of the Falkirk Wheel. It was such a nice feeling as we approached the aid station, which was also the finish line. In the pouring rain, all four of us walked hand-in-hand to record our marathon finish. We did it! We were officially a marathon family as mum, Mekaal and I completed our first marathon to join the 150 plus marathons that dad had completed. Our aunt and grandma were at the finish line, waiting for us. The organisers gave us warm soup, and we headed to the main race headquarters to receive our finisher medals and certificates. We had another lovely surprise there; a sports massage treatment. We quickly showered and changed before jumping on to the massage table. I was in so much pain that I did not want the therapist to touch me at all; it felt as if someone was jabbing me with knives. Conversely, my dad and mum greatly enjoyed their massages and looked so relaxed. After all that, we headed home, and all I remember is going straight to bed. I was crying with pain, but I remembered what my dad always told me. *"Pain is temporary, but pride is forever."* The next morning, I woke up sore everywhere, but I was happy that we had crossed the first hurdle. At 11-years-old, I was a marathon finisher, while my brother had completed his first marathon well before his tenth birthday! The next day, my dad returned to Qatar, and we went back to doing what normal nine and eleven-year-old kids usually do during the summer holidays.

CHAPTER 5

CONTINENT NO. 2
ASIA (DNF)

QRS FALL EDITION – RACE 3
Friday 10 November 2017
Doha, QATAR

We returned to Doha in late August, a week before the start of school. The worst time to be outdoors in Qatar is from August to early October, as it is not only hot, but humidity is close to 80%. On the other hand, the weather in North America, Europe, and even the southern hemisphere is ideal for running so most marathons are held there during either the spring or autumn seasons. Dad could have scheduled races for us during this time, but he did not want us to miss school. The weekend in Qatar is Friday and Saturday, so we would have missed at least two days of school if he had scheduled a Sunday marathon anywhere in the world. So, the plan was to tackle the second marathon in Qatar as part of Qatar Running Series. The remaining races were planned during our school holidays.

Qatar Running Series has multiple distances from 3 km to a full marathon. Most runners in Qatar sign up for shorter distances; mainly 10 km, 5 km, and 3 km. The main events start at 6 am, and the prize ceremony is held around 7:45 am. Marathon runners have to start at 1:30 am while half-marathoners start at five. This ensures that everyone is able to finish the race before the prize ceremony.

As we settled into our school routine, our daily schedule was wake up at six to be at school by 7:15 am, return from school by 3 pm, followed by extracurricular activities, homework, dinner, and bed by nine. Since returning from Scotland, we had been training regularly for longer distances and mixing running with football, karate, and swimming. So, our cardiovascular systems were prepared to take on the next marathon.

The advantage of doing the Asian leg of the challenge in Qatar was that we neither had to fly anywhere nor did we miss any school. However, there was one problem, and that was to get to the start line at 1:30 am. A few days before the race, our parents tried to get us into a routine where we would be in bed by 8 pm. However, that failed miserably as our body clocks weren't aligned to sleep that early. I remember we were both wide awake until ten and would try and sneak into the kitchen for water or something to eat. The plan just wasn't working. On Thursday night, we had an early dinner and dad's instructions were to make sure we hit the sack by 7 pm. We did as we were told but were just too anxious and excited about the race, which kept us awake even longer than usual. I still remember checking the clock before I dozed off; it was 11:15 pm, and in about an hour we were going to be woken up and driven to the race start. Both our parents had decided to run with us. Since dad was organising the event, he left even earlier to set up the course.

I was right in the middle of a dream when the dreaded alarm clock went off. A few minutes later, mum walked into the room and turned the lights on. I couldn't even remember what she said before going back to her room to get ready. The next thing I recall,

I was at the start line, in a strange place, and Mekaal and I were waiting for the start gun to go off. I heard mum's voice again in the background, and as I opened my eyes, I was still lying in bed. Gosh, another dream! It was quite the mission to get both of us out of bed; we were not in a happy place. Exhausted and disgruntled, we quickly changed, had something small to eat, and were in the car at 1 am driving to Education City and the race start. No-one spoke a word on that fifteen-minute journey; mum was as sleep-deprived as we were. I knew it would not end well.

We arrived at Oxygen Park, where other marathon runners, including dad, were waiting for us. We quickly collected our bib numbers and were ready to pound the pavement at that ungodly hour. The course was a 7 km out-and-back loop, and we had to do it six times to complete the marathon. Each and every turn was familiar as we had run that course over 50 times during the QRS events. Mum, even with the lack of sleep, was determined to complete the marathon with us. Mekaal and I both started out at a decent pace and had completed the first 10 km in an hour. However, by 15 or 16 km, we were beginning to feel the pain. I slowed down considerably while Mekaal stayed with mum. My head was spinning, and I felt like throwing up. That's when dad looked at me, asked a few questions as we ran together, and told me to stop. I didn't want to disappoint him, so I told him that I would do another round to see how I felt. With so much marathon experience under his belt, he knew something wasn't right. Our conversation went something like this:

Dad: *"Zara, how are you doing?"*

Me: *"Not too good."*

Dad: *"Zara, what day is it today?"*

Me: *"It's Friday. Why are you asking me silly questions?"*

Dad: *"How long did you sleep for last night?"*

Me: *"Maybe one or two hours."*

Dad: *"Sing the four times table."*

Me: *"Dad, I am too tired to do that."*

Dad: *"Do you want something to eat or drink?"*

Me: *"No, if I eat something, I will throw up."*

Dad: *"OK, here is the deal; you are stopping at the half marathon mark."*

Me: *"Why? I can carry on!"*

Dad: *"No, it's too dangerous. I cannot let you continue."*

Me: *"So, that means we will not be able to break the world record?"*

Dad: *"Of course you will; we just need to find another race. I don't feel comfortable with either of you continuing now."*

With that, it was time for us to call it quits. In hindsight, of course, it was a good decision as I somehow knew we could not have continued. In fact, as dad was driving us home, we both slept in the car.

Mum and dad both ended up completing the marathon. We were disappointed because we had quit halfway. Later that day, dad told us about a few races where he had decided to quit himself. In 2015, he was running his 100th marathon. He had specifically planned it in Doha so his family and friends could come to cheer him on. It was a big occasion, and we were all looking forward to seeing him reach his dream of 100 marathons. However, he wasn't feeling well during the race and decided to quit at 31 km. He said he listened to his body, and that's why he quit. A week later he flew to Luxor, Egypt, and easily completed his 100th marathon there.

For us, this DNF (Did Not Finish) turned out to be a good life lesson. There may be times when we need to cut our losses to preserve our bodies. We knew we would come back stronger next time. Our parents warned us that when we grow up, we will face similar situations in life. Sometimes, it is better to step back and analyse a situation, rather than rashly tackle it head-on. Tough situations demand analytical thinking. So, in the end, the Asian leg wasn't completed, and we returned to the drawing board. We had three tough races coming in December, and we had to be ready for those!

CHAPTER 6

Continent No. 2
South America

MAGELLAN MARATHON
Thursday 14 December 2017
Punta Arenas, CHILE

Since the failed attempt in Doha a month earlier, we were both a bit nervous about the two upcoming marathons in South America and Antarctica. With the amount of money our parents had spent on getting us to the bottom of the world, a DNF was not an option. However, they comforted us by saying that there is nothing more precious in the world than human life. If they thought our life was in danger during any of the upcoming races, they would pull us off the course. Mekaal and I did not want to disappoint them, and we made sure we were in top physical fitness for these two events. We had been made aware of the challenges we would face in both Chile and Antarctica, so we were also well prepared mentally to expect the worst and hope for the best.

It was my dad's sixth adventure to the cold continent, so he knew very well what lay ahead for us. He even knew each and every turn and the gradient of both courses and explained them to us in detail, so we knew what to expect. This was important, so we at least knew how to pace ourselves and tackle the terrain.

Just getting to Punta Arenas at the southern tip of Chile, was more than a marathon in itself. We took the 15 hour, non-stop 7 am flight from Doha to Sao Paulo, Brazil. Since it was a day flight, we hardly slept and instead binge-watched movies. Upon arriving in Sao Paulo, we were exhausted, and that was not even half the journey.

After immigration, we headed to the transit lounge where there was a five-hour wait for the next flight to Santiago, the capital of Chile. We arrived in the Chilean capital after 2 am and by that time, we were flying or in transit for 24 hours. Needless to say, we were all grumpy and jaded. I just wanted the travel to end and to sleep in the comfort of a hotel bed.

However, there was yet another five-hour wait in Santiago before the next flight to Punta Arenas. Luckily, we found a nice pizza place inside the terminal and decided to eat and rest there for a while.

To catch the flight to Punta Arenas, we had a ten-minute walk to the domestic terminal, which was lovely with plenty of comfortable sofas, and we all managed to sleep for a few hours. Thankfully, dad woke up just when they were announcing the last call. So, we frantically gathered our belongings and rushed to the gate to get on the plane. It was a close call, but it was all part of the adventure. The flight to Punta Arenas was about four hours, and we flew south over the magnificent Andes, home to majestic peaks and glaciers. Due to climate change, it is predicted that the glaciers will melt in the next 20 to 40 years, which would be drastic for locals who rely on fresh water. Over 40 million residents are expected to be affected in the years to come due to the fast melting of the glaciers. We were glad to see them then as they may not exist when I return as an adult.

Chile is an unusual country geographically. Looking at the world map, it resembles a skinny leg and a foot. The country has over 6,500 km of coastline and is only 200 km wide, sandwiched between the Pacific Ocean in the west and Andes Mountains in the east. To the north is the Atacama Desert, with its awe-inspiring landscape. It is both the driest place and the oldest desert on earth. Chile also has over 1,300 volcanoes, the most in the world, and most of them are active. The country also boasts five UNESCO World Heritage sites, including the famous Easter Island. The oldest mummy in the world, dating back to 5050 BC, was also discovered in Chile. For us kids, we also discovered the longest swimming pool in the world, as confirmed by Guinness World Records, is situated in Algarrobo city. It is one kilometre long and was completed in 2006. I surely want to visit there another time.

However, for this particular trip, the focus was on completing the marathon. At around 9 am, we finally landed in Punta Arenas. It had taken us almost 40 hours to reach our destination, the gateway to Antarctica and Torres Del Paine. During the journey, we experienced three sunrises, but no sunset. As we exited the plane, collected our baggage, and walked out of the terminal, we had our first experience of the cold southern breeze. It was our first trip to the southern hemisphere; Singapore was the nearest we had previously been. A DAP representative, the organiser of both marathons, was waiting for us in the arrivals lounge. We sat in a van, and they drove us to Hotel Cabo De Hornos in downtown Punta Arenas. It is a luxury five-star hotel overlooking the famous Plaza de Armas, known for the statue of adventurer Ferdinand Magellan. Before embarking on the voyage to Antarctica, all tourists pay a visit to the statue and kiss his feet for good luck!

We had to wait a few hours to check-in, as guests from the previous night had not yet checked out. We were in interconnected rooms, which meant Mekaal and I had full privacy, and we could watch TV and chill without disturbing our parents. However, we were too exhausted and took a nap instead. In the evening, we met up with other runners and had a nice four-course meal in the hotel restaurant.

Marathons in Antarctica are heavily dependent on the weather which can change on a dime and flights can get cancelled for days if the visibility is not good. Dad knew this all along as he has been there so many times. While we were relaxing, he was busy communicating with DAP to find out what the situation was. All we knew was that we would not be flying the next day, and we took full advantage of the situation and decided to do some local sightseeing. Our first stop was the Cementerio Municipal "Sara Braun", a beautiful cemetery built in 1894. As we walked through the impressive entrance, we arrived in a labyrinth of beautifully manicured trees leading up to graves the like of which I had never seen before.

Some of the mausoleums were bigger than our house. I wondered how rich the people must be who were buried there. We walked around the complex that was spread over four hectares of land. It was simply out of this world. Dad told us there is a similar cemetery in Buenos Aires, only bigger and perhaps even more impressive than this one. Anyway, for us, it was an eye-opener. On the way back, we stopped at a quaint café in downtown and had the most amazing churros and hot chocolate.

On the morning of our third day in Punta Arenas, we received news that the weather was still bad on the cold continent and all flights were cancelled. Therefore, to save time, we were advised to run the Magellan marathon that day. We were not ready for that, but we knew we needed to be flexible. We quickly changed and were ready for the race, which started opposite our hotel inside the park. The course was designed in a way that we would pass through most landmarks in Punta Arenas during the first lap. After that, it would be a short 5 km out and back loop on the Punta Arenas promenade. Lucky for us, the sun was out, and we got into a good rhythm for the first part. The views of the Southern Ocean with a cooling breeze blowing was refreshing.

The running path went all the way up to the naval museum. After that, we ran on the sidewalk. We first passed by the Nao Victoria Museum and continued running towards the shipping dock, which was the turnaround point of the first lap. On the way back, the wind picked up, and it became overcast. Punta Arenas weather, as dad said, is unpredictable.

The weather can change very quickly once it becomes cloudy and strong winds from the Southern Ocean start blowing. I could see Mekaal was beginning to struggle, and so did mum. Dad noticed it and decided to stop at the gas station where we all sat for five minutes and enjoyed a hot chocolate and some biscuits. After gathering enough energy, we decided to move on. For the next 15 to 20 km, it was a combination of run and walk. However, at around the 30 km mark, I hit the wall. My legs were stiff, and I was cold. I needed an energy boost and possibly a second wind to get me to the finish line. What we had initially decided was that everyone would remain together for the whole race and we would support each other. I felt bad as I was holding everyone back. Mekaal and mum had managed to find a good rhythm and were motoring along. At one point, mum looked at me and told me to toughen up and run. She was getting upset as she wanted to complete the race as soon as possible, and I was slowing her down. At that point, dad intervened and told Mekaal and mum to go ahead and that he would stay with me. For the next six or seven km, dad and I ran and walked together. He took my mind off the race by telling me stories of his marathon escapades and all the interesting and funny things he had encountered. During this time, I found my second wind and started running. We both ran at a decent pace and caught up with Mekaal and mum who were surprised to see us. By then, we were only a few kilometres from the finish line and decided to finish the race together. It was a great feeling as we laughed, made fun of each other, and crossed the line to record our second continent completion. After the DNF in Qatar, our morale and confidence reached a new high, and we were proud of what we had achieved. After the evening dinner, we were presented with our finisher medals, and we went straight to bed.

The Southern Hemisphere adventure was only half done. We still had the Antarctic race to complete, and our trip was dependent on Mother Nature. There was nothing we could do but wait for good news.

Displaying our finisher medals after completing the race in Chile

CHAPTER 7

Continent No. 3
Antarctica

KGI CLASSIC MARATHON
Saturday 16 December 2017
King George Island, ANTARCTICA

The good news came a day later when we were woken up by a phone call at 7 am. The DAP team were calling to inform dad that the weather was clear to fly to the cold continent and that they would pick us up in an hour. It was a mission getting out of bed with sore legs, but we managed to get changed, had breakfast and were in the lobby ten minutes before schedule. Thankfully, we had packed all our Antarctic gear the night before and moved the remaining suitcases into the hotel's storage room.

Before heading to Antarctica, all travellers must attend a mandatory trip briefing. We had ours the day we arrived in Punta Arenas at the DAP office, in a cosy little conference room. The team had prepared delicious finger food for us. A DAP agent first showed us a documentary on Antarctica, followed by all the do's and don'ts when we arrive at King George Island (KGI). It was extremely informative, and one takeaway from the meeting was that we were not allowed to throw anything on land as it may contaminate and harm the local wildlife. I certainly didn't want the penguins to suffer. Mekaal and I were already in love with them even before seeing them in real life. After the hour-long meeting, all the adults were offered pisco sour, the famous local cocktail from the Peru and Chilean regions. Mekaal and I were content with orange juice. Once we left the conference room, they handed us the Antarctic gear which we had to wear upon arrival in KGI. It included a red jumpsuit, welly boots, and various other giveaways like scarves and headbands. We chose the smallest sizes, but they were still big for us. I guess they don't get that many kids travelling to the region. But we were happy with what we received and were now looking forward to the trip, especially seeing the penguins up close and personal.

The van arrived at 8 am sharp, and we met the driver in the lobby. I was nervous but excited about the upcoming trip. Once we reached the airport, we were handed our boarding passes and advised to head through security. The airport was busy with flights operating to all parts of Chile and Antarctica. The Antarctica queue was long as they had a backlog of four days due to poor weather. We discovered that most of the travellers were flying to Antarctica to catch a cruise ship from there. They were all going on the big plane, but for us, dad had booked an exclusive charter as a surprise.

After clearing security, we went straight to the airport's private lounge and relaxed in the comfy sofas. I asked mum why some people are allowed in the private lounge while others sit outside. She told us that she and dad have a platinum card which allows free access to lounges around the world. Equipped with computers, games, magazines, and all-you-can-eat food and drink, we made ourselves comfortable while waiting for the flight announcement.

An hour or two passed, and I saw dad looking a bit worried. He was constantly in touch with various staff members. He then came and told us that our plane had a mechanical problem and they were getting another plane ready. The anxiety grew with every passing minute. There were other people stuck as well, and there was a lot of commotion in the lounge. At around noon, after waiting for almost three hours, we were given the go-ahead to proceed to the gates. It was finally getting real, and I had butterflies in my stomach as we walked towards a small plane parked 50 metres from the gates. I had never been in such a small aircraft, and just the thought of flying over the Southern Ocean in that toy was unnerving. Getting on board took a mere three steps.

The DAP plane that flew us over the Southern Ocean

Mum, at six feet tall, bumped her head on the ceiling as she nervously settled into her seat. There was barely room for nine people, and that included the two pilots. The interior was nothing like any other plane that I have flown on. We quickly took our seats and fastened the belts. I was sitting beside Mekaal while mum was holding on to dad as if she were on some rollercoaster ride in Alton Towers. The pilots were extremely nice and friendly and assured us that we were in safe hands. A few minutes after settling in, the propellers started spinning, and for the first time, I experienced what pilots do when they are about to take off. They both had headsets on and were communicating with the control tower, and they checked all the buttons a few times, toggling them up and down before the plane started moving forward. We quickly gathered speed, and before I even realised, we were up in the air. I had never seen a plane take off that quickly; perhaps because it was a small plane and did not need a lot of runway space. As we gained altitude, I looked out of the window and admired what lay beneath. We were at the very tip of South America and flying towards the unknown. Within minutes, we were above the Southern Ocean. From then on, there would be no land for the next three hours, barring a few small islands.

The Southern Ocean is one of the roughest in the world. Dad once took a cruise from Ushuaia to Antarctica on a research vessel and told us about the Drake Passage; a body of water so rough that the average wave size is anywhere between 30 and 50 feet on a typical day. Back in the day, when there was no Panama Canal, ships used to circumnavigate the Magellan straight and Cape Horn to sail from the Pacific Ocean to the Atlantic Ocean. In the process, vessels would get destroyed in the rough seas. The reason for the rough water around Cape Horn is the Antarctic Circumpolar Current that flows from west to east around the continent of Antarctica. It keeps the warm ocean water away from Antarctica, which helps maintain its ice sheet.

Luckily for us, we were flying over all this and had an excellent visual of Cape Horn from 30,000 feet above the ground. About half an hour into the flight, we all started to relax and enjoy the view; miles and miles of blue water with no land in sight. I asked dad if this plane could glide if something went wrong. He just smiled and said that if we landed in the water, the chances of surviving were virtually none. The water is so cold that hypothermia would set in within minutes and we would become a nice meal for the Orcas down below. I saw mum stiffen up as she heard the conversation.

Just when I was wondering if there would be any food served during the flight, our DAP staff member, who was accompanying us on the plane, started handing out lunch boxes. It was not an ordinary flight lunch tray; instead, the meal was served in a silver tin box with a DAP logo, and a picture of a cute penguin. Our names were even on the boxes, which was cool. Apparently dad had told DAP what we all liked, and they had customised the lunch for us. The box contained a mix of raw vegetables, chicken sandwiches, dessert, juice, and water. Mekaal and I devoured our meals as if we would not get another one any time soon. While eating, I noticed one of the pilots taking pictures from his cell phone and laughing. He then turned around and said if we looked up, we'd see the other DAP plane on the way back from Antarctica. We got into a little Q&A session with him, which was awesome as you cannot do that on any normal flight.

Me: *"So, how do you know what altitude to fly at to avoid a collision?"*

Pilot: *"We always fly 1,000 feet lower when flying out than when we come back."*

Me: *"Have you ever landed this plane on water?"*

Pilot: *"No, never, but we can glide and land safely. By the way, are you really going to run a marathon in Antarctica?"*

Me: *"Yes, that is the plan. We're going for a world record attempt."*

Pilot: *"Wow that is amazing. I can't run more than a few kilometres!"*

There was no time for more conversation as the control tower contacted the pilot, and a few minutes later, we were asked to fasten our belts for landing.

We had our first sight of Antarctica as the plane slowly descended towards King George Island. From up above, all we could see were glaciers and some rock formations. It was fascinating to see the island where we would be starting our marathon. The advantage of being in a small plane was that we could watch the landing from the cockpit as well as the side windows. As we descended, I noticed how much ice there was on the island. The Collin's glacier, which occupies 98% of King George Island, was directly beneath us, basking in all its glory under the clear sky. The pilot made a U-turn over the island to align us for a perfect landing. This was my first time seeing a pilot land a plane, and I had the best view. We flew between the jagged rocks and landed on the gravel runway. Phew! We made it! Though it was a perfect flight with no turbulence, we had all been a bit on edge during the entire journey, not least because we were in a small plane flying to the coldest continent on earth.

Upon landing and stepping outside, we felt the cold breeze which instantly froze my nostrils. It had been snowing for a week, and ours was the first plane to land in over seven days! Dressed in our red jumpsuits, welly boots, gloves, and beanies, we were escorted to a truck that would take us to the Russian base. I did my "walk like a penguin" impression as I strolled towards the truck which had chains like on tanks rather than tyres.

So there we were, all huddled together, as the truck crawled up and down the hills towards the base. Dad looked concerned as he told mum this was the most snow he had ever seen on King George Island.

During the ride, dad spoke with the DAP team who had already marked out the course for us. It was a slightly shorter loop than usual, since part of the course was under thick snow and therefore too dangerous to run on. Most marathons here take place between late January and mid-March, summer in the southern hemisphere when the winter snow usually melts away. However, we had arrived before the summer solstice, and it was more like spring, waiting for the winter snow to cascade into the ocean. We reached the Russian base, "Bellingshausen Station," after a ten-minute ride. The base, set up in 1968 and one of the first on the island, was named after the 19th-century Russian Antarctic explorer, Fabian von Bellingshausen.

King George Island is unique in every sense. On the map of Antarctica, it is on the northernmost part of the peninsula which forms part of the South Shetland Islands. It is 95 km long and 25 km wide with a land area of 1,150 square kilometres. The island was discovered in 1819 and named after the then King, George III, by the British explorer William Smith. Since then, the island has been claimed by many countries, including Chile in 1940 and Argentina in 1943. However, the USA and Russia do not recognise these claims. Currently, many countries have research stations on the island, including Russia, Argentina, Brazil, Chile, China, Peru, South Korea, Poland, Uruguay, and the USA. The majority of these stations are permanently staffed, researching areas as diverse as biology, palaeontology, ecology, and geology. So, in a way, the island is similar to Qatar when it comes to population diversity, but not the weather. In 2013, dad's favourite rock band, Metallica, performed on the island. He said everyone had to wear headphones as they did not want to disturb the wildlife, which includes three species of seals (Weddell, leopard, and elephant) and three species of penguins (Adélie, gentoo and chinstrap). The flying birds on the island are mainly limited to the skuas and southern giant petrel. We were eager to tour the island and view the wildlife, but for now, the focus was on why we were here.

It was around four when we entered the living quarters. The entire base was nothing more than a huge steel container providing accommodation for around 15 scientists. We walked through the long, narrow corridor to the common room that served as the race pit stop. There was a TV, microwave, computer, and fridge with tables and sofas. We were welcomed by the head of the base, an elderly Russian glaciologist who had been stationed on the island for over 30 years. He was shocked to hear that my brother and I were going to run a marathon on the island.

There was no time to waste as we had to start the race as soon as possible. Before the event, we all decided we would run an ultramarathon (50 km) instead of the full marathon (42.2 km). Other runners had signed up for an ultra, so instead of having two race distances, we decided to go all out for the 50 km. After all, what was the probability of a nine-year-old boy and eleven-year-old girl ever again attempting an ultra in the Antarctic? That record, if we were able to complete the distance, was likely to stand for a pretty long time. So, the course was measured, eight loops of 6.25 km each, from the Bellingshausen Base to the Great Wall base and back. We were ready at the start line at 5 pm. After the usual few pictures, the DAP agent sounded the horn and off we went. The first 100 m of the course was slightly downhill towards the docking station. From there, we followed the road up past the Chilean base, and on to the top of the hill.

Start line picture before the 50 km ultra-marathon

With all the snow that had fallen, we were on two feet of fresh powder in certain parts. Happily, we were well dressed, but our trail shoes were not fully waterproof. They were water-resistant, which does not help much when ploughing through a few feet of soft snow.

At that point, we did not care much as our legs were fresh, and we were keen to see some penguins. Dad had told us to conserve energy in his pre-race briefing. What he meant was to walk up the hilly parts and run on the downhill.

Tough running conditions due to snowfall over the previous few days

As we walked up the big rise towards the Chinese base, we remembered that this dreaded hill would need to be conquered no less than 16 times during the race. It was clear this would not be a piece of cake. As we reached the top, dad advised us to stop for a minute, take a breather and enjoy the beautiful views the island had to offer. He said this would be the only time we would appreciate the views, as, on subsequent loops, our happiness would shift to moaning and complaining. Standing there we saw the majestic Collins glacier overlooking the bay, with hundreds of feet of blue ice. On the right was a round white balloon kind of structure and further down were some more buildings in pink and red colours. That was the Chinese Great Wall base and the turnaround point of the course. Standing on top of the hill for a minute was important, as we finally understood the course and the challenges we would face during the race. At least I had a plan of how I would tackle the course. Descending was a breeze as we sprinted down the half muddy, half snowy trail to sea-level. From there, the remaining route was flat by the sea towards the turning point. My brother and I were happy that there would be no further hills. Right then, I noticed dad wearing his sarcastic smile, which usually meant there was trouble ahead. So another conversation began between dad and Mekaal. For once, I stayed quiet.

Mekaal: *"Dad, this looks easy. We like this course, and it is not that bad."*

Dad: *"Are you sure that it's easy?"*

Mekaal: *"Well, there are no hills, so definitely easier than the first part."*

Dad: *"Looks like you forgot the pre-tour briefing that I gave you when I explained the course in detail."*

A few minutes later, it dawned on us what he had meant about the underfoot conditions close to the Chinese base. As we passed the first Chinese sign, I felt as if a sharp object had gone through my running shoes. I looked down and noticed how the course had changed. It was all jagged rocks and pebbles. Not only that, but the running surface was also uneven. Every step we took, our foot slipped and sank a few inches into the gravel. It seemed as if the ground was one giant magnet pulling us down every time we pushed forward. We ran about a kilometre along the bay until there was a left turn sign beside a huge rock. That road led us to the Great Wall base, but it was not an easy path. Right beside the rock, the gravel path was blocked by a few feet of snow which could not be avoided. It had turned to ice, so we had to be very careful; one mistake and we would have either slipped into the bay or injured a leg. Dad, as usual, took the role of Sherpa and guided us across the 20 feet long stretch of ice. Again, this had to be tackled 16 times.

After about 30 minutes, we reached the Chinese base. It was right next to the natural pond that was home to at least a few dozen skuas. I remembered watching '*Happy Feet*' as a young kid, and the scariest birds were the skuas who prey on baby penguins. I was finally able to see them up close and personal. The skua is a brown coloured bird which looks like an eagle but has feet like a duck which help it float in the water. They are extremely territorial and can attack humans if threatened. One of the lessons on the pre-tour briefing was to avoid venturing off the main road because birds could be nesting. Since Antarctica has no trees, birds nest either on the rocks or ground. Upon reaching the Great Wall base, we made a U-turn to head back to the start at the Russian base. Of all the bases we saw on the island, the Chinese was most impressive; they seem to have invested a lot of money there. On the way back, an SUV approached us in the distance. As it neared, we saw a Chinese team of four waving at us from inside the vehicle. They looked surprised, and a bit puzzled as to what a couple of young kids were doing in that cold, snowy weather. We simply waved back and pushed on towards the start line. By this time, I had realised this would be the biggest challenge of my life. Running was not an issue for us but dealing with the elements was not easy. Completing 50 km on the cold continent with high winds, below-freezing temperatures, an uneven trail, and multiple layers of clothing were just some of the challenges.

Around 100 metres before turning towards the hill, mum shouted, *"PENGUINS!!!"* We looked towards the bay and four cute little penguins were waddling on the ice. It was surreal; I finally got to see a penguin in the wild. At that moment, we did not care about the race. Instead, my brother and I just stood there with wide-open eyes admiring the flightless birds as they continued their march towards the clear blue sea.

Finally meeting the penguins!

We took a few pictures; then it was time for us to continue our trek towards the Bellingshausen base. For the next twenty minutes, we were happy and did not realise that we climbed over the hill and started our descent. After almost an hour, we were back to where we had started. This was just the first loop; we had seven more to go.

Before starting our second loop, dad checked to see if we were warm enough. We took a few sips of water, a piece of chocolate, and off we went. The second time around was unlikely to be as exciting as the first one, so we did not waste time stopping to take pictures or admiring the scenery. However, we did pause for a few minutes to say hello to our penguin friends. By that time, there were six of them, and they had walked much closer to us beside the road. My brother was eager to pat them, but we had been given clear instructions not to touch the wildlife unless they chose to come near you. A couple of the birds started following my brother, and it just made his day. He slowed down until they caught up to him, then they turned and waddled back towards the bay. Dad told us how, when he had visited Antarctica for the first time and was on a penguin-watching day trip, a baby penguin had come and sat on his lap, fallen asleep and started drooling. We, on the other hand, had an ultra to run so we continued pounding the trail towards the Chinese base.

During the run, we were checked continuously by mum and dad to see if we were alright. After completing the third loop, mum gave us some cookies and a painkilling syrup. The plan was to complete circuit four then head back to the base to use the washroom and get something warm to drink, which we did almost three and a half hours later. The DAP team had prepared hot chocolate, soup, and warm cookies for us. It was so lovely and warm inside that I did not want to leave. By that time, we had completed half the distance, but still had another 25 km to go. At that point, mum looked at dad in disgust and said:

"Whose bright idea was it to run an ultra? Isn't a marathon enough for you?"

I think she was getting irritated by going and back and forth on the same route, especially near the Chinese base due to the stony terrain. Mum is the bravest woman I have ever known. Sports, especially long-distance running, do not come naturally to her. However, she would do anything to support us in following our dreams. A few years back, she had been diagnosed with lederhosen disease, a condition that affects her feet and hands. The condition is aggravated when she exerts herself for too long, like walking and running. I could tell she was in a lot of pain during that race, especially when running over the jagged rocks near the Great Wall base. Imagine having a tumour on the ball of your foot, then being told to run on rocky terrain for 50 km. Well, that's what she had to endure, but she hid her pain and kept on encouraging us.

After finishing the hot chocolate, we were ready to venture out into the cold again and continue the run. Dad and Mekaal were ready, but mum and I had to make a bathroom stop, so the boys went ahead. As I walked out of the washroom, I noticed something was not right. My trail shoes were wet, and when I tried putting them on, they felt a little smaller. I realised that Mekaal had accidentally run off in my shoes. Great! Now what to do? There was no way I was going to wait another hour for him to come back and exchange the shoes, and I couldn't run in his shoes. It was an honest mistake as our shoes were the same make and colour, but mine were one size bigger. Mum came up with a solution and told me to put on the big welly boots and walk the loop instead of running. This way, I would cross Mekaal at some point along the course and tell him what an idiot he was. About 30 minutes into the walk, I found the idiot running back towards us from the Chinese base with dad.

Me: *"Mekaal, you are wearing my shoes!"*

Mekaal: *"No, I am not! These are my shoes."*

Me: *"Really! Check again!"*

Mekaal: *"Look, they are mine, it says seven,"* as he raised his shoe to show me the sole.

Me: *"Exactly, I am size seven; you are six."*

Mekaal: *"Oops, I did not know."*

He then looked at my big, goofy welly boots and burst into laughter.

Mekaal: *"You should run in those; at least you won't feel cold!"*

Me: *"Ah, NO! I want my shoes back!"*

Our parents intervened, and it was decided that Mekaal would go back, change into his shoes, and leave mine at the entrance. So, here I was doing a full loop of the course in welly boots. After a while, I got comfortable with my new footwear and developed a brisk walk which helped me conserve my energy. At the end of the loop, I finally recovered my trail shoes. In hindsight, it was a bad decision as the shoes were damp and got even wetter as I continued my run. It was around 10 pm, and the conditions underfoot had changed for the worse. The snow was beginning to melt, creating puddles along the course. Halfway down the loop, my feet were soaked, and it was starting to get cold. With the wind chill, the temperature had dropped to minus ten degrees centigrade, and we still had more than 15 km to go. I was not thinking straight, as we all continued our runs and walks without speaking to each other. Mum was visibly exhausted and in a lot of pain. She hardly ever cries, but this time she couldn't hold back her tears. Dad wanted her to stop, but she refused, knowing that Mekaal or I may well give up too. I stayed with mum and Mekaal and dad ran the penultimate loop together. On the turnaround, we caught up with them. By then, I did not want to talk to anyone and just wanted to finish the race. Dad tried to chat with me, and this is how it turned out:

Dad: *"Zara, are you OK? Can I get you a chocolate bar?"*

Me: *"No, dad, I am not OK."*

Dad: *"Do you want to continue? You're almost done with the full marathon."*

Me: *"I don't care about the full marathon; I just want to finish what we started."*

Dad: *"Great attitude! You may be in pain now, but you will enjoy your achievement later."*

Me: *"I don't care about the stupid race, or the stupid distance, or the stupid world record. I just want to finish and go back."*

I think dad realised there was no point trying to talk further, so he quietly stayed behind and walked with mum. At least he knew I was determined to finish the race. Mekaal soon joined me, and we walked up the hill towards the Russian base. Not a word was spoken for the next 15 minutes as we reached the base to start our eighth and final loop. We had already completed the marathon, but it was one last push back towards the Chinese base and back again to make it 50 km. I swear that was one place I did not want to see again in my life. It was already past midnight, but since we were in Antarctica during the longest daylight period of the year, we saw the sunset and sunrise within two hours.

We reached the Chinese base for the last time and turned around, taking a breather and giving each other high fives. We were only three km from the finish and between us, and the end was just one big hill. We had conquered that hill 15 times. It had demoralised us, but we wanted to have the last laugh. So for the final time, Mekaal and I decided to run up that hill to send a clear message: *"We beat you, Mr Crazy Hill. You lost to a couple of nine and eleven-year-old kids!"* In hindsight, it was us who seemed crazy, not the hill. It sapped every ounce of energy from our bodies, but we still had the last laugh. After that, it was downhill all the way back to the base. Mum and dad joined us, and we all ran the last 500 m together to complete the ultra. Even though it was past 1 am, the DAP team members were there to cheer us on as we crossed the finish line.

It took a while for it to sink in just what we had achieved. Mekaal and I had just broken three world records. Not only did we break the world record for the youngest male and female to compete in a full marathon in Antarctica, but we also set the record for the youngest to complete an ultra-marathon on the cold continent. The third record was for the youngest siblings to complete an ultra-marathon in Antarctica. As dad said, these records will not be broken anytime soon! Only time will tell if any other crazy siblings will challenge these records.

After completing the ultra-marathon in Antarctica

After resting for a bit, we were told that our dinner was ready at the main base. Tired, cold, and starving, we made our way to the cafeteria. Just the thought of a warm, hearty meal made me happy again. We were so hungry we could have eaten a whole pizza or a big, juicy burger. However, to our disappointment, there were only a couple of cold boiled eggs, a garden salad, and a few loaves of bread. We couldn't believe what we were looking at! The chef had gone to bed as it was past 2 am, and the DAP agent could not provide anything else. We later found out that the chef had been told we don't eat pork and immediately assumed we were vegetarians. We can all laugh about it now!

After dinner, we were asked to collect our bags from the base and walk to our accommodation, which was the only "hotel apartment" on the island. What we didn't know was that it was at least a kilometre away and we had to climb 100m up a hill. So, there we were, climbing a steep snowy hill to our shelter after completing 50 km and eating a cold, vegetarian meal. We got there at just past three am and were pleasantly surprised at how nice the accommodation was. It was a two-bedroom apartment with three bunk beds in each room. There was one bedroom for our family and a second one for the other runners who had accompanied us. There was also a kitchen, bathroom, and living room. Mekaal and I quickly grabbed the top bunks, and within minutes all four of us were out for the count. No one bothered to change or even brush our teeth; we were too tired to think of anything else. Just as I tucked myself into the warm sleeping bag, I wondered how my brother and I had managed to pull this off. I was excited and relieved that we had both completed marathons on two continents within a few days! I know how happy my parents were, especially dad, who had paid so much money for the whole family to come on this adventure. Thankfully, we did not let him down!

CHAPTER 8

SIGHTSEEING IN ANTARCTICA

"Good morning, kiddos!!!" I have always hated that greeting ever since I started school. Well, guess what, here it was again and this time in Antarctica, of all places.

"C'mon dad, I am tired. Let me sleep," as I buried my head under the warm sleeping bag.

"Well, we are taking a zodiac to a penguin colony island, then going on a trek to watch elephant seals. So, it's your call!", said dad as he started packing up to leave the apartment.

I so wanted to have another hour of snoozing, but the thought of missing out on an adventure of a lifetime got me out of the bunk bed and into the living room where everyone was having breakfast. No one spoke much as we were all exhausted, but we enjoyed a decent selection of jams, cheeses, and various breads. Our accommodation was beside the Holy Trinity Church, the southernmost Eastern Orthodox Church in the world and one of eight churches in Antarctica. Since we had an hour before the tour start time, we decided to visit the impressive structure as it's a must-do excursion in Antarctica. Not only that, but it's also the most beautiful building on the island; a 15m-high wooden structure built in the old-fashioned Russian style. It is not that big on the inside but can still accommodate up to 30 worshippers. We were told that the structure was built out of Siberian pine, and had been dismantled then taken by truck to Kaliningrad. From there, it was shipped to King George Island by the Russian supply ship Academician Vavilov and reconstructed on top of the hill. That, to me, sounded like a lot of work. The church is open year-round, and along with Russian, it also holds services in Spanish for other nationalities. There is one permanent priest who lives on the base who we got to meet and spend time with that day. In 2007, there was even a wedding service, probably the first one on the continent.

On our return, a truck was waiting to take us down to the bay. We had a whole day of sightseeing planned and Mekaal and I were so excited. We were given life jackets and asked to board the zodiac, which is a small inflatable black boat with the motor at the back. Soon, we were out on the cold blue sea passing small icebergs on our way to the penguin island, which we reached around 20 odd minutes later. Dad had warned me about the smell, and he was right. I love the penguins, but not the sight and smell of their poop. They eat so much krill that it turns their guano a pinkish colour. I saw on a BBC documentary that their guano is even visible from space. Anyway, apart from the unappetising discussion about their droppings, the birds are, indeed, quite fascinating. They followed Mekaal and me wherever we went, and dad took plenty of close up photos of us playing with them.

Around mid-day we were back in the main Russian base; this time it was packed with scientists, and there was a buffet laid out for us with fresh pizzas, chicken, rice, vegetables, and salad. The food hit the spot, and we were ready for the trek to the elephant seal colony. I was glad we had plenty to eat as we had to walk for over an hour through knee-deep snow, with a bit of rock climbing and a descent into the bay. What we witnessed upon arriving was surreal. Elephant seals, as the name suggests, are humongous and they lay on the beach in their dozens soaking up the sun on a bright, Antarctic summer's day.

We tried to get close to get some pictures before trekking along the beach to find fur seals and a couple of leopard seals. All the pain from running two races on two continents quickly vanished. On the way back, Mekaal and I even had a snow fight, reminding us one we'd had in Iceland a year earlier.

Our flight back to Chile would be at 11 pm, so we had another seven hours to kill in Antarctica. The DAP team invited us to the Chilean base to meet with their team and get our passports stamped. It was so cool to have an Antarctica stamp in our passports. They even had a store selling Chilean wine which they offered to all the runners. Obviously we did not partake, but the other runners enjoyed it and ended up buying some to take back home. From there, we went souvenir shopping where dad bought an Antarctica magnet, and we bought some postcards to mail to our cousins back home.

Our remaining time in Antarctica was spent inside the Russian base with the friendly scientists. They invited us to play ping-pong and mum played the Russian version of Ludo. It was such an awesome feeling to be with strangers who spoke no English but still made us feel at home. The Russian priest we had met earlier in the church was somewhat of a sports enthusiast. He played ping-pong with dad and Mekaal then later played cards with mum and other scientists.

One of the glaciologists invited Mekaal and me to his workplace where he spoke with us about climate change and how it is affecting the continental ice. Dad later told me that what we experienced on this trip would never be possible with a bigger group. On his previous trips to Antarctic marathons, he had slept in cold tents and never did much sightseeing as the excursions cannot cater for big groups.

Moreover, none of the other marathon runners could enter any of the bases. We were just so privileged to see and do all that we did in that fascinating place.

At around 10 pm, we headed to the runway as the plane was approaching. It was so cool watching it land. This time we were on a regular flight with other passengers heading back to Chile. I think it was a 60-seater but only had 15 people aboard. As we took off, I looked down and said goodbye to Antarctica. In a little over 24 hours, Mekaal and I managed to run an ultra, visit penguin and seal colonies, play ping-pong with a Russian priest, learn about glaciology from an expert and had an awesome pizza at the base. Most people wait a lifetime for such experiences, and we did it before we even became teenagers. With that thought, I must have dozed off, as next I knew we had arrived at Punta Arenas.

The mission was accomplished, and we had checked off two more continents in our quest to complete seven marathons on seven continents by March 2018. Now it was time to do some sightseeing in Chile and Brazil as we had another five days before returning to Qatar.

CHAPTER 9

ROBBERY IN CHILE AND A MISSED FLIGHT TO RIO

Upon landing in Punta Arenas after midnight, we were driven back to our five-star hotel. All we wanted was a warm shower, change of clothes, and a long nap, and indeed that's what we did. That night I slept like a baby knowing there were no marathons to run or flights to catch for a few days. Next morning I was woken by the jarring noise of bags and cases being opened and closed. Dad looked upset. He kept checking the bags, then the cupboard, then the bags again. I had no idea what he was doing, but mum also looked worried.

"What's wrong?" I asked while I could barely open my eyes.

"*Dad lost all the money,*" mum answered.

"*Huh, what money?*" I enquired.

"*Well, there was extra money in the suitcase which we left in the hotel storage, but it's not there now,*" said mum, shaking her head.

Dad didn't say a word as he headed down to inform the hotel management. The whole day was spent dealing with hotel staff who checked all the video footage of anyone entering the luggage area and even our hotel room over the last few days, but nothing concrete was found. Dad was advised to go to the police station and file a complaint. I don't remember the amount, but it was enough to pay for our trip to Rio and more days of sightseeing in Chile. So, mum, Mekaal, and I spent the entire day relaxing in the hotel, which was OK as it was raining outside anyway. The next day we were looking forward to a planned trip to Torres Del Paine National Park with the other runners. However, when dad got back from the police station, he said he had to return the next day as the papers needed to be signed by the chief of police who hadn't shown up for work that day. That meant the national park trip had to be delayed by another day. Dad didn't want to dampen the holiday spirit, so he decided we should enjoy our time in Chile as if nothing had happened. He found an ATM and withdrew enough cash for the rest of our trip.

Next day, while everyone else left for Torres Del Paine, we walked to the Nao Victoria Museum. It is a private, open-air museum built to showcase replicas of various ships that contributed to the discovery of the Magellan region, its colonisation, and its historical significance. The replicas were made using traditional shipbuilding techniques. The first ship we saw was *Nao Victoria*, arguably the most famous in the history of navigation. She was part of the fleet commanded by Ferdinand Magellan who discovered the waterway around the southern tip of continental South America. She was later used for and became the only ship of five to complete, the first-ever circumnavigation of the globe. Strolling inside the ship made me wonder how they could have crossed rough seas over 500 years earlier. She looked tiny compared with the cruise ships we spend one week holidays on in the Caribbean and Europe. Back then, they did not have luxurious sleeping cabins, washrooms, a dining room, or above all, on-board entertainment. I was so glad I was born 500 years later so I can enjoy all the comforts the world has to offer today.

Before embarking on our Antarctic trip, dad had shown us the movie, *Shackleton*. He remains the most famous explorer of the 20th century and was known for his excellent management skills. Shackleton saved his entire crew after their main ship, *Endurance*, was crushed by sea ice. To seek help, he used an unfeasibly small boat, the *James Caird*, to sail to South Georgia over the cold and rough Southern Ocean. I simply could not believe my eyes when I saw the replica of the *James Caird*. It was not more than 12 feet long and two feet wide, and he managed to find South Georgia in it, without the aid of GPS. I sometimes consider how tough and smart people were back in the day. Compared with their heroics, my marathon run in Antarctica pales in comparison.

The third replica in the museum was *HMS Beagle*. It was a British ship that sailed in the Magellan region for over three years, and the crew included Charles Darwin. *HMS Beagle* is the famous ship on which Darwin started developing his theory of evolution. So, we spent the day going back in time to see what life was like in the past. Though I have the utmost admiration for those brave souls, I would certainly not like to live in those times.

Perhaps people will say the same thing about us 500 years from now! Later that evening, we had a lovely meal at Luna Café and dropped off a QAR 5.00 bill with our names on it. It's a café tradition that global visitors pin a small denominated note from their country on the walls. We had an early night as the next day was our big trip to Torres Del Paine national park.

The alarm was set for 5:30 am as the bus was due at seven. It was a long drive, over 300 km each way, so, we would spend most of the day on the bus. Luckily, we had downloaded movies and music to our iPads. The bus was on time, and after collecting a few other visitors along the way, we headed north on a long, lonely highway called *Chile Route 9*.

There wasn't much to see except wide-open plains and some wild llamas; so mostly we remained engrossed in our devices. Our first stop was Puerto Natales, about 250 km from Punta Arenas. It is the gateway to Patagonia and more importantly, Torres Del Paine and we were transferred to smaller vans for a more personalised experience. En route to the park, we made a quick stop at Mylodon's cave, discovered over 120 years ago by a German explorer who found an animal skin inside. The hide belonged to a large, pre-historic sloth-like animal called Mylodon that died more than 10,000 years ago. There is a statue of the animal inside the cave, and it looks pretty scary.

It was a fairly short drive from there to the park. The scenery was breath-taking with lakes on one side and tall mountains on the other. On entering the park, we drove for a few miles until our first sighting of Torres Del Paine. *Torres* means tower and *Paine* means blue. In other words, blue towers that looked utterly majestic from all angles. The three towers rise to 8,200 feet above sea-level and are a sight to behold on a clear sunny day.

Torres Del Paine National Park

With the group, we walked to a natural waterfall then hiked up to another observation point to view the beautiful peaks. The wind was relentless as we half-climbed and half-fell sideways. I even saw one kid pushed back a few feet as his parents watched in disbelief. It was a great experience, but we didn't want to stay too long. We now had two hours to ourselves for more sightseeing. What Mekaal and I wanted most was a hot chocolate and some cookies, and we found both in the comfort of a warm, cosy café. Mum and dad wanted to take us over a suspension bridge through the forest. We were up for it and joined them straight after finishing our drinks. It was quite a magical experience, walking through the jungle and crossing the bridge over a river. We even scared mum by jumping at either end of the bridge while she was in the middle! It reminded her of the Carrick-a-Rede rope bridge in Northern Ireland. Back then, we were babies and had to be carried over the swinging bridge in crosswinds.

Dad and I carried on to the long, black sand beach without realising that mum had turned back as Mekaal wanted to go to the bathroom for number twos. He often seems to be in this situation at tricky times and in awkward places. Once, he had to do the same while we were climbing a mountain in Ireland. After a long walk and very interesting chat with dad, we reached the restaurant and reconnected with mum and Mekaal. We had seen it all and were tired, so we wanted to head back to Punta Arenas, though the thought of spending another three and a half hours on the bus was quite painful. In the end, the journey turned out to be a lot longer than we anticipated. First, we had a flat tyre which had to be changed. Then, half an hour later, the traffic came to a standstill as the road was closed due to a landslide. The driver had to go back to the national park and take another route to Puerto Natales. Unfortunately, the problems did not end there. As we arrived at the bus station, we were told the scheduled bus we were supposed to be on had already left for Punta Arenas. It was past 10 pm, and we were exhausted. Somehow, the tour company arranged some small vans for the stranded passengers, and we were herded onto them for a three-hour journey back to Punta Arenas. If you have ever seen sardines in a can, that's what we resembled. Dad kept his cool and reminded us of some of the journeys we had taken when we were young kids. Once, he explained, we boarded a bus from Phnom Peng to Siem Reap, and for five hours we had sat on our parents' laps on a crowded bus. Dad had taken plenty of these off-the-beaten-track bus rides around the world, so this one did not bother him one bit. We reached our hotel way after midnight and went straight to bed. It was our last day in Chile, and we were looking forward to spending the last three days of our trip in Rio de Janeiro before finally heading back to Doha.

Mekaal is a big football fan, and most of his favourite players are from Brazil and Portugal, so, it was a big thing for him to visit the Maracana Stadium in Rio. Mum was looking forward to a stroll along Copacabana and Ipanema beaches, while I wanted to climb up the mountain to the Christ the Redeemer statue, having seen it in the movie Rio when I was younger. Dad had visited Rio in 2010, but the statue was getting a facelift then. As we flew to Santiago over the majestic peaks of the Andes, we were ready to change into shorts and T-shirts. The chilly climates of Antarctica and Patagonia were taking a toll on our bodies, and we needed some warmth on our bones. We landed on time, but as we headed to the international terminal for the flight to Sao Paulo, there was a delay. Initially, we were told the delay was only an hour, but that changed, and we ended up waiting for three hours. By the time we got to Sao Paulo, our plane to Rio had already left. You can imagine the difficulty of getting a replacement flight during the Christmas break. Dad tried for hours at different airline counters, but no joy, so finally he returned to our original airline, and they gave us three nights' accommodation at an airport hotel with all meals included. So, there it was, the last part of our trip was spent in a city it felt that no one wants to visit and has nothing amazing to offer. We met up with my parents' friends, Nadine and Semjon, a German couple who worked at the embassy. We knew them from the Hunza marathon which dad had organised in Pakistan where they had been posted. They took us out for a lovely traditional buffet at *Churrascaria Vento Haragano*. The restaurant serves fresh cuts of regional meats.

The chef brings large skewers to your table and cuts the meat before placing it on your plate. They kept bringing new items every few minutes until we had to ask them to stop! The food was delicious, and there was also a huge salad bar and ice cream stall. It really made our day. Afterwards, we visited Ibirapuera Park in downtown Sao Paulo before heading back to our hotel. The final day of our trip was spent inside the hotel. We were all exhausted and ready to head back home.

Two weeks previously we had arrived after a 14-hour flight from Doha, and now as I boarded the Qatar Airways flight and sat beside my brother, I recalled the whole trip in my mind and realised what we had achieved, and the new things we had learnt in those two weeks. Surely, no textbook or school syllabus in the world can teach you all that. I can only thank my parents for this.

The world record attempt was not even halfway done; Dad hadn't yet told us where the next marathon would be. As we were flying over the Atlantic, dad came and sat beside me:

Dad: *"So, are you ready for your next adventure?"*

Me: *"Ah, no. I am tired. Is it in LA at the end of next month, when we have school holidays?"*

Dad: *"Unfortunately, no. It is in four days"*.

Me: *"What? Where?"*

Dad: *"Well, get ready; we are flying to South Africa for the weekend!"*

Me: *"No way! How long is that flight?"*

Dad: *"About nine or ten hours."*

Me: *"Oh! C'mon, dad. That's tiring!"*

Dad: *"Well, we don't want you guys to miss school, so it's best to do it now. Besides, we'll be flying back to Doha on New Year Eve. So, when the year changes from 2017 to 2018, we'll be on the plane!"*

Me: *"Really? That's so cool!"*

At that moment, Mekaal interrupted with a one-liner, *"So, Zara, we will go on a plane in 2017 and land in 2018. I will tell my friends we were on a plane for over two years!"*

We all had a chuckle, and then it was time to get some rest. After a 13-hour flight, we were back in Doha on Christmas Day, jet-lagged and preparing to fly out again in a few days!

CHAPTER 10

Continent No. 4
Africa

RUNNING FESTIVAL OU RONDAWEL
Saturday 30 December 2017
Pretoria, SOUTH AFRICA

The race in South Africa was an unplanned one. Originally, we were due at the Ile-Ife marathon in Nigeria, which is organised by a friend of my dad's. However, his passport had less than six months on it, and he couldn't get a visa. So, the plan was scrapped, and the search began for another race in Africa. It would have been easier had we joined him for the Southern African Challenge five months earlier as we could have chosen one of the seven countries in which he was organising events. But, as they say, hindsight is 20/20. Finding a race in Africa is not easy, and more so a race where they allow kids to take part. Dad contacted loads of race organisers, but liability issued stopped us participating. The rule in South Africa, so we heard, was that only runners over 18 could participate in road races. Typically, dad, perhaps one of the best researchers in the world, did manage to find a race director who would allow us to run. The plans had only been finalised while we were in Sao Paulo and he had booked our flights on 23 December. Mum was exhausted and had scheduled business meetings, so she did not join us.

There is another rule in South Africa that we learned from some South African friends of my parents when we reached Doha. If one parent is leaving South Africa with their children, written consent has to be provided by the other parent and needs to be stamped by the South African embassy in the country of residence. Since we arrived in Doha on Christmas Day, naturally the embassy was closed. Mum called the embassy the next morning and after a long wait was able to get in touch with consular services. As luck would have it, the embassy was only open for one more day, December 27th, before being closed across the New Year holidays. So, they told mum to head over quickly with all documentation to get the letter approved and signed. She did not waste any time and was at the embassy gate five minutes before opening time. The document was signed, and we were good to go. It was a close call, but as always, 'Team Rahim' crossed that hurdle.

On the evening of December 28th, we were all packed and ready to head to Hamad International yet again. We only needed a hand-carry each, since it was just a two-night trip. Mum drove us to the airport, and instead of stopping at the usual gate two, which is exclusively for Qatar Airways, she went further and stopped in front of Gate four.

"Dad, weren't we supposed to stop back there?" I enquired.

"No, we are not flying Qatar Airways this time," he said with a smile.

"Then what airline are we flying?" I asked.

"ETHIOPIAN AIRLINES...YAY" he laughed as he tried to make it as exciting for us as he could.

"*EWW,*" I said, with an air of a snobbish disgust.

I must admit travelling on Qatar Airways has spoiled us. We love their five-star service; other airlines just don't cut it for us. According to dad, Ethiopian Airlines is the best African airline in the world. It was his first time on it too, but for him, it wasn't an issue. He has been on planes where there wasn't even a toilet!

"Don't be a snob and get moving," he said quietly as we walked towards the check-in counter. Ethiopian Airlines did not have a direct flight to Johannesburg, so we had to change planes in Addis Ababa. We boarded the first flight, and it looked like the aircraft had been built when my grandparents were my age. The upholstery needed a makeover, the tray table was dirty, there was no entertainment system, and the whole plane shook as we took off into the night sky. The flight was around four hours, so we tried to catch some sleep. Dinner was served after an hour, and it was surprisingly tasty. Dad always told us about how good Ethiopian food is. In Toronto, he used to go to a shack with his friends that served cheap and delicious Ethiopian food. Even though I am a very picky eater and Mekaal never eats on planes, we both had small helpings and agreed with dad.

We disembarked in Addis Ababa and were bussed to a small terminal which looked as dated as the plane. The place was jam-packed with one modest restaurant serving tea and snacks. We waited in the lounge for about 20 minutes before our departure was announced. To our surprise, the next plane was top class, similar to Qatar Airways jets. It had inflight entertainment with loads of movies, the stewardesses were extremely friendly, and their uniform was so elegant. They wore a long, white gown, similar to a shalwar kameez and very different to other airline uniforms. The food was again delicious, and soon after eating we all dozed off, only to be woken up just before landing.

We were greeted in arrivals by the owner of the guest house dad had booked online. This was something new for us as I never expected an owner to come all the way to receive us at the airport. Dad has been to South Africa many times and told us how friendly the locals are. However, he warned us about the crime in Johannesburg and other big cities. The country has seen its fair share of violence over the last few decades. Before 1991, the country was boycotted by most of the world due to apartheid. However, things changed when Nelson Mandela took over the country. After visiting South Africa, I came back and watched the movie *Invictus*, which indeed was an eye-opener for me.

After a 15-minute drive, we reached a big, fully gated house with barbed wire and a security system. Everyone has to protect their home like this due to crime in the area. We were greeted by the staff and shown our clean and well-decorated room. The owners had two dogs; one a massive German shepherd and the other a cute little poodle. Dad and I share a fear of anything that moves and is not human. Mekaal, on the other hand, loves animals and he didn't waste much time befriending the dogs. He was out playing ball with them while I stayed in the room with my equally cowardly father!

The day's plan was to chill in the guest house before driving to Pretoria next morning for the race. We were hungry, so the owner's wife offered to take us to the nearby shopping complex where we could get something to eat. The one place that stood out was *Chicken Licken,* a KFC style franchise serving greasy chicken, fries, and soda. Instead of Colonel Sanders, there was a picture of a rooster. What the heck, we were running a marathon next day, so we may as well put some diesel in our bodies. Besides,

Mekaal is a junk food addict. Just like KFC, fried chicken places always smell delicious, and the first bite is heavenly, but by the time you finish the meal, you don't want to go back anytime soon. That's how we felt, so we decided to walk home as that was the only way we could digest the food. The evening was spent relaxing at the guest house with a light dinner and lights out at 8 pm.

We packed our bags early the next morning and were about to head to breakfast when I saw the big, monstrous dog sitting in the main hall, wagging his tail. Dad and I stopped as if we had seen a ghost. Mekaal just looked at us, shook his head, and walked out to move the dog away. *"Nice teamwork, Mekaal"*, I grinned. Over breakfast, we discussed our race plan. I didn't know at that point that the race we were running had started three days before and would continue past New Year.

"What kind of race is that?" Mekaal asked while still a bit shocked. *"It's a multi-day ultra-event. There are different distances. Some people run for six days, some for three while others do 100 km, 50 km, 24 hrs, 12 hrs, 6 hrs or simply a marathon,"* said dad in his classic never-ending sentence-style.

"OK, hang on, do people actually run non-stop for six days?" I asked if I heard him correctly.

"Yes, quite a few of them do. But they obviously take breaks for food and a quick sleep then run again," dad explained.

"Oh, so are we going to run for days too?" Mekaal asked with a worried look on his face.

"Hahaha, no, we signed up for a 12 hr race, so our job would be to complete the marathon within 12 hours," clarified dad.

"But what if we complete the marathon in less than six hours? Will we still need to keep on running for 12 hours?" asked Mekaal.

"If you want to, sure, keep on running. I will go and sleep in the tent once I've done my 42.2 km" dad said in a sarcastic tone.

"Yeah, right, we will all stop then," and I closed the topic.

Our ride arrived an hour after breakfast; the race director had arranged for one of his staff members to drive us to Pretoria over an hour away. On any longish drive, dad always explains about the place we are in or heading for, and this ride was no different.

Dad: *"So kids, not many people know this, but Pretoria is one of the capital cities of South Africa. This is considered unique, as most countries have just one capital city. But South Africa has three, or rather the government branches are divided among three. They are Pretoria, Cape Town, and Bloemfontein."*

Me: *"Why is that?"*

Dad: *"I think it's from back when the Union of South Africa was created. There were conflicting views on which city should be the capital, so they came up with this compromise to keep everyone happy."*

South Africans call traffic lights robots. I don't know why, but it made me giggle the first time I heard it! I wondered what they call those machines that we call robots! There are many other amazing facts about South Africa. For example, they have the longest stretching wine route in the world. They are the largest producer of meat in Africa and love a BBQ which they call *Braai*. The highest commercial bungee jumping bridge in the world is in South Africa, and finally, the country has 11 official and many more unofficial languages. This eclectic mix of cultures gave South Africa its nickname the *Rainbow Nation,* which is also embedded in their national flag. Hmm, the joys of travelling, we learn new things every day!

The time passed quickly, and before we knew it, we were off the highway and driving along small roads. A few minutes later, we reached the race park. The course was a dirt track and flat as a pancake, and we could see runners on it. On either side of the track were tents, presumably for runners who were doing multi-day races. The race director, Eric Wright, greeted us warmly and took us straight to the tent he had prepared for us. It was roomy and comfortable with three beds. Our initial plan was to start the race in the evening to avoid the hot sun. However, almost the entire course was shaded, so we decided not to waste time and start immediately. We were given bib numbers with a chip attached at the back. The course was 500m, 250m out and back. Therefore, to complete a full marathon, we had to complete 85 loops. Just the thought of running 85 times around an out and back loop made me dizzy. But it had to be done, so there was no time to complain.

We started the race around 3 pm and felt good going back and forth. It wasn't humid, and we were well protected from the sun, so there was nothing to worry about.

Every time we passed the turnaround and went under the timing antennas, our race stats would show up on the big monitor overhead. Other runners on the course were really nice and friendly. We would see them repeatedly, and they would smile and sometimes give us a high five. By 5 pm, we had already covered closed to 20 km but were beginning to feel hungry as our last meal had been breakfast. Dad had already organised dinner for us, and the event team was cooking it onsite. Just the smell of food being cooked made us even hungrier, but we had to wait, so we kept running and walking to cover as much distance as we could. Finally, on our 50th loop, we were called in by the race director. The food was ready, and we were famished. Thankfully, it was a home-cooked pasta lasagne with salad and fresh bread, not processed chicken. We sat down and started eating. A runner who we first met briefly when we had arrived came and sat beside us. He had long hair and an even longer beard and looked like someone who had been stuck on a desert island for years. Dad looked at him and asked, *"So, are you the real Forrest Gump?"* Typical of dad to ask an embarrassing question, but he laughed, and we all had a great time eating and chatting. He was from Sweden and had run over 1,000 marathons around the world. He was injured, so was only walking this time, but was going to walk for six straight days with three hours sleep every day. My jaw dropped when I heard him say this.

It was beginning to get dark and we still had another 17.5 km to go. We knew we would cover the distance within 12 hours given our time so far, even if we took three hours additional break or even crawled for part of the course.

But we were determined to complete it quickly and get a good night's sleep. So, for the next hour, we walked so our food would digest. It was really nice chatting with Mekaal and dad as we talked about everything under the sun, and even made plans for our next trip to Los Angeles. As night fell, the trees surrounding the course filled with birds. One particular tree reminded dad of the Alfred Hitchcock movie *The Birds*. He had seen it as a kid and subsequently developed a phobia of birds; he cannot be in the same room as a bird. The tree was completely full of birds, and not ordinary ones but the size of full-grown eagles. As it was dark, we could not tell the species, but they looked seriously vicious. One runner heard us talking about the birds, and he reassured us that they would not attack, as it was his third day running the same course. That was quite a relief, and we motored along, completing loop after loop. When we were about 7 km from the finish, Mekaal started to limp as his calves were tight. I was also getting tired, so we asked dad if we could sit outside the tent for a little while. Realising we were both tired, he decided to massage our calves. Oh, that felt so magical, and I just didn't want him to stop. Anyway, after a five-minute break, we were out again and kept on doing the loops as darkness fell, with only a few lights every 30 m on the course. The organisers had to turn off the hard rock 80s music they'd been blaring all day, as quite a few runners were already sleeping. Just after 9 pm, Mekaal completed the marathon distance, followed by dad. I, however, had two more loops to go as I had been to the washroom during the race while the others continued. Mekaal and I had made a pact that we would finish all races together, so he ran with me until the finish, and we sprinted across the finish line together. I had completed 42.5 km while

Mekaal ended up running 44 km. It was a fantastic feeling as we had completed the fourth continent. We were exhausted, though, and our tent was only 50 m from the finish line. All we wanted was to crash, and we did exactly that. There was no strength left in us to walk another 100m to the communal washrooms for a shower or even to brush our teeth. Instead, we opened the sleeping bags, slid our bodies inside, and that was good night!

I slept straight through and was woken by Bon Jovi's classic *Living on a prayer*. We were all groggy and wanted to sleep a little longer, but yet again, we had a plane to catch. Stinky and tired, we showered, changed, and ate breakfast. An hour later, Eric did the prize distribution ceremony for the finishers where we were presented with finisher trophies and caps. They were lovely and something different from the usual finisher medals. Moreover, I loved the South African hospitality. The people are really nice, friendly, and make you feel at home. Speaking of home, that's where we were heading. The cab driver drove us straight to JNB airport, and we boarded the flight back to Doha via Addis Ababa.

Proudly displaying our awards after completing the race

An hour before landing, we crossed into 2018 and Mekaal got the biggest kick out of that. I know he was longing to go back to school and tell his friends that he flew on a plane in 2017 and it landed in 2018. Oh well, whatever makes him happy! We were glad to be back in Doha and mum came to meet us at Hamad International. It was so lovely seeing her again, but we had missed her running with us. I guess we had to get used to that, as she was not able to accompany us on the remaining events due to her work commitments.

CHAPTER 11

Continent No. 5
North America

ROCKIN' THE BAY MARATHON
Sunday 28 January 2018
Long Beach, CA, USA

This was one race I was really looking forward to. Actually, that's a lie, as I never look forward to any race. The truth was that I wanted to visit Los Angeles. Why, one must ask, LA of all places? Well, because I grew up watching American shows, be it sitcoms, reality TV, music, or movies. Along with sports, my other interests include music, acting, and making YouTube videos. I don't have any desire, at least for now, to pursue acting as a career, but I do love performing on stage. In Qatar, I am a member of *Hummingbird*, the premier acting school in the country. LA is the production home for most of the US entertainment industry, so combining a trip with visits to motion picture studios and running a marathon was a no-brainer.

Again, LA had not been the first choice, because it was a 16-hour flight from Doha. Dad had initially tried to register us for a race in Florida. However, once again, we were refused entry because of our ages. In the winter of 2014, dad had decided to break a fifth Guinness World Record. After completing marathons and ultra-marathons on all seven continents, he wanted to break the record for the most ultra-marathons completed consecutively. At that time, the record stood at ten ultras in ten days. Dad discovered a race planner by the name of Charlie Alewine who organises around 50 marathons a year in Long Beach, California. During the holiday season, he holds a back-to-back, seven-day winter series. Dad signed up for that and flew to LA for two weeks to run 50 km every day. He broke the record by completing all 14 ultra-marathons in 14 days. While in LA, he became good friends with

Charlie and spoke very highly of him when he returned to Qatar. Guess what? Charlie proved how great he was again when dad approached him after four years with a request to allow us to run his race. He was thrilled to hear from dad and immediately approved our participation. Moreover, the race date fitted perfectly with our school break as we were off for a week in late January. This meant that we would have five days in LA to run and sightsee. Mekaal and I simply couldn't wait to catch that flight, but all this was a month away, and we had school and other extracurricular activities to do. On 10 January 2018, Mekaal reached double digits, and we had a cool party for him. Apart from being a gifted athlete, he is a really kind, caring, and friendly kid. After all, how many kids are there in the world who have completed a half, full, and ultra-marathon before the age of ten? On the local circuit, he is always on the podium in triathlon, aquathlon, and running events. However, his first love is football, and he takes his practice very seriously.

On Saturday, 27 January 2018, we boarded the plane to LA. It was a 16+ hour direct flight leaving Doha at 7 am. Again, a day flight is always the toughest as we are usually wide awake but tied to a seat for all those hours. Thanks to the excellent Qatar Airways entertainment system, I managed to watch at least four movies and a few sitcoms. Mekaal and dad slept a bit, but I stayed up as we flew over ten time zones to reach LAX. It was almost midnight in Doha when we landed, but in LA it was early afternoon. After an hour in the rental shop, we drove out with an upgraded Jeep Grand Cherokee. On the hour-long drive to Long Beach we were so exhausted that both of us slept in the back. Dad had booked the hotel closest to the race start; it was on a major intersection surrounded by restaurants and shops. The room was clean and had a good wifi connection. Right beside the hotel was a fast-food chain called *Jack in the Box* which I had never heard of, but since we were tired, we walked across the parking lot and went straight in. It was, I would say, a glorified McDonalds with a bigger selection of burgers and sodas. The fries were tasty too, and I thought they were way better than some of the other fast food joints I have tried. It was 5 pm when we finished, and Dad had asked us to stay up for another hour so that we can get used to the new time zone. However, both dad and Mekaal were snoring away within three minutes. In the middle of the night, I noticed dad moving around and typing on his smartphone. He was wide awake, and so was I.

"Dad, are you up?" I whispered so that I didn't wake Mekaal.

"Yes, wide awake. I had a good sleep," replied dad.

"What time is it?" I asked as it was pitch dark outside.

"It is 1 am. We all had about eight hours sleep," he replied.

"I slept well too, Dad," Mekaal said as he woke up and joined in the conversation.

"What time is the race?" I asked

"It's a 5 am start, so we need to be there by 4:45 am at the latest to collect our bibs", dad said as he turned the lamp on.

"Oh, so what shall we do for another four hours?" Mekaal asked as he wanted to get up and run.

"Well, we can watch some TV and get something to eat," replied dad.

"Do you think there will be anything open at this time for breakfast?" I asked sarcastically.

"I think Jack in the Box is open 24 hours," dad replied.

"Oh, that again. OK, we should get some breakfast from there then," I said as I headed to the washroom.

The burger joint was closed, but the drive-thru' was open, so dad walked round there and tried to order, but was told they couldn't serve a customer who isn't in a car! Dad told us the story as he walked into the room to collect the car key, over which we had a good chuckle. Twenty minutes later he was back with a giant breakfast. Since there were more than three hours before the race, it was the perfect time for us to carb-load our systems.

By 4:30 am we were dressed and ready. The mornings were a bit chilly in LA, so we had our running T-shirts plus a light fleece to keep us warm at the start. Marina Bay was just a five-minute drive away, and dad knew the terrain. He had run six of his 14 ultra-marathons here and assured us that we would love the course. It was pitch dark as we parked the car and walked to the start line to collect our bib. We were greeted by a friendly group of runners and support staff who knew in advance what we were aiming for. Charlie was very nice and welcoming and had laid out a great aid station with Gatorade, bananas, oranges, and some savoury comfort food. Dad already knew a couple of runners, so they got into a long conversation. One of them, Alberto Perusset, is a police officer and a barefoot runner. Dad told me that he knows a lot of movie stars as he provides security during the Oscars. His Facebook page has his photo with Clint Eastwood and lots of other celebrities. There were about 25 runners at the start line, and the race started promptly at 5 am. It was still dark, but the streetlights were on. The course was a 5.25 km loop, so we had to complete eight loops. The weather was ideal for running, and we got into a good pace. Dad stayed with me while Mekaal paced the faster runners. We couldn't see much, but I could tell we were running between a lake and some beautiful houses.

A few kilometres ahead, we crossed a bridge and ran beside a park until we reached the turnaround. On the way back, we ran around a housing complex, which led to the start line. It was not a straightforward course, and there was a fairly high chance of getting lost. I think that scared dad as Mekaal was on his own while running through the estate. As we finished the first loop, dad asked Charlie if he had seen Mekaal and he nodded. Phew! Just before the bridge, we saw a kid walking a bit funny. As it was still dark, we couldn't tell who he was, but dad recognised the walk. It was Mekaal, so we ran faster till we reached him.

Dad: *"What happened? Why are you limping?"*

Mekaal: *"I fell during the run and lost my way too."*

Dad: *"I knew it. I told you to stick with me for the first loop so that you know the course."*

Mekaal: *"Yeah, I know, but I want to run and finish the race faster, dad."*

Dad: *"Are you hurt?"*

Mekaal: *"No, I am OK."*

Dad: *"Good, then stay with us, and we will run together and enjoy ourselves."*

Me: *"Yes, Mekaal, let's chat. It's a nice day to run, and the course looks amazing!"*

Mekaal: *"OK fine, you slow coaches."*

For the next hour, we ran non-stop, covering a good distance. It started getting brighter, and the scenery changed dramatically. The lake on our left looked spectacular with many beautiful boats parked in the marina. It looked like a very affluent area of town with stunning houses overlooking the lake and the park. For the next loop or two, we just admired our surroundings. Running beside the lake and marina with tall palm trees, sailboats, parks, and stunning housing estates was a treat. Everything looked so green and tidy. I wished the other races we ran were as easy and beautiful as this one.

By 7:30 am, we had completed the half marathon and were not at all tired. I think we could have run faster but, why? We were not going for any podium records, so it was better for us to maintain a good pace and finish under the seven-hour cut off time.

On every loop, we would see the same runners who would smile and wave at us. The park was getting busy too, and we saw plenty of people doing yoga, Zumba, and other fitness classes. The sailboats were out as well, and it just seemed like a fun place to live with so many active people on a Sunday morning. I always imagined California to be a trendy place full of fit and healthy people and for what I saw that day, I was spot on with my imagination.

After 9 am, the course became busier as we saw a big group of 5 km and 10 km starters. There were some kids as well, probably our age, who were running with their parents. One of the ladies who dad knew from the last time he ran Charlie's races started running and chatting with us. She said her kids are so lazy that they are still sleeping and won't wake up till she gets back home after the marathon. *"I am going to go back home and tell them I met these wonderful kids who flew 16 hours from Qatar yesterday and ran a marathon today,"* she said as she wished us well and continued with her race.

The end was near as we turned past the start line for the eighth and final time. We were a little over 5 km away from the finish.

Mekaal and I grabbed a juicy watermelon and some Gatorade from the aid station and proceeded towards the lake, marina and the park for one last time. The sun was out in full force by that time, and it was getting a bit warmer. We didn't care as our legs felt OK. Just after 11 am, we made our final push to the finish line. Dad ran ahead and asked us to slow down so he could take a video of us crossing the finish line. After crossing, we were greeted by a dozen or so people, and huge medals were handed out.

To this day, Charlie's is the largest medal that we have received. Mekaal and I thoroughly enjoyed the race, and we thanked everyone before driving back to the hotel. This was continent number five completed with only two more races to go. We were two races away from getting the phone and PS4. But right then, that wasn't what we were looking forward to. Universal Studios and a trip to downtown LA were on our minds.

After showering, we headed to a Chinese restaurant for lunch. We were sick of fast food, so we wanted to eat something wholesome. The meal was tasty, but we were getting a little tired due to jet lag and the marathon. So, we relaxed in our hotel room for the afternoon. By 6 pm, we were snoring away. Sleeping that early meant we would again wake up at an ungodly hour, and dad would have to go to *Jack in the Box* to get us a greasy breakfast at 3 am. Well, that did happen, and my poor dad had to make that 100 m trip to the drive-thru' again to pick up coffee, bagels, hash browns, and orange juice. I am sure he didn't mind as we had completed the marathon and held up our side of the bargain.

That day, we decided to stay in to recover from the race as we knew the following day we would need a fresh pair of legs for all the walking we had planned in Universal Studios. In the afternoon, a movie director visited to interview dad for Fiona Oakes' documentary "Running For Good". Fiona is a vegan runner and holds multiple Guinness World Records. She and dad have run some of their toughest races together. They first met during "Marathon Des Sables", the 250km race through the Sahara Desert, and then did the North Pole and Triple 7 Quest. Dad keeps challenging Mekaal and me to do "Marathon Des Sables" with him when we turn 18. Our answers remain "no" no matter how many times he asks. In fact, our other deal with him was that we would never run another marathon until we are over 18. Later we went to a Japanese buffet. The food selection was so huge that it took us five minutes to walk around the restaurant to decide what we should eat. They had live cooking stations with lobster, shrimp, BBQ, and a large spread of salads and desserts. We were so stuffed afterwards that we didn't need dinner. Our jet lag was improving as we delayed our bedtime till 7 pm.

CHAPTER 12

HOLLYWOOD AND THE VOMITING EPISODE

Universal Studios, Hollywood

The day I had been waiting forever since dad declared we would run the North American leg of the marathon in California had finally arrived. After a 5 am start and a Dunkin'

Donuts breakfast, we were ready for the hour and a half rush hour drive to Universal. The traffic problem in Los Angeles is well known, and there is no way to avoid it. From Long Beach, we were stuck in bumper-to bumper-traffic all the way to the studios. As it was a winter weekday, the park was open from 10 am to 5 pm. However, we had booked our tickets online, so we were allowed inside an hour before everyone else. Anticipating the place would be busy, we wanted to complete as many rides as possible before the park opened up to the general public. On the way to Universal, I had my first glimpse of the famous Hollywood sign on the hill. We reached the studios at 8:50 am, and surprisingly, it wasn't that busy. We busily planned our activities in detail after collecting the park map. We aimed to cover the most in-demand rides early and tackle the other ones later. Dad had visited Universal Studios in 1989 when he was 15 years old, and he wanted to see if Knight Rider was still there. Back then, it was the most followed series in the world and he sat inside the car and had a chat with the onboard computer K.I.T.T. When he returned to Pakistan, he shared the pictures and stories with his friends. Walking through the park, it looked so different to him, and rightly so as his visit was almost 30 years ago.

Our first ride was Harry Potter, and there was no queue as we entered Hogwart's School of Witchcraft and Wizardry through the winged boar gates. In summer and during school holidays, the average waiting time for this ride is over an hour. It is a 3D ride and we had to wear special glasses. As our feet dangled in the air, we had a complete 360-degree experience as if we were part of the production. The broomstick fight scene was as real as it could get. The ride was so amazing that I wouldn't have been happy to wait an hour for it had I visited the park during summer. I am a big Harry Potter fan; I've read all the books and watched all the movies. We even walked through Hogwarts Castle and saw the "Moving Portrait Corridor" and "The Portrait of the Fat Lady" just like Harry Potter and his friends did!

Jurassic World was next, followed by *Revenge of the Mummy* and *Transformers*. All the rides were excellent; however, the best and probably the most informative was the *Studio Tour*. In a tram, we visited various studios where actual movies are shot. In between these were 3D rides built into other rides. We even experienced an earthquake, or what would happen if King Kong tried to bring down the bridge we were on, or what it would be like to come in close contact with *Jaws*. It all felt so real. Dad said the 3D rides didn't exist when he had visited the park, but he was glad to see Knight Rider parked among the old cars in a forgotten spot during the studio tour. I think it made his day, but what he had admired as a cool sports car back then just looked like a piece of junk 30 years on! After lunch, we visited more rides and even had our pictures taken with animated characters, including the cast of *Despicable Me, Snoopy, The Simpsons,* and many more. We also watched a live stunt show, *WaterWorld,* which was fantastic. By 3 pm, we had completed all the rides in the park, so we decided to do the best ones a second time.

Chilling with Madagascar team!

That trip to Universal Studios was truly memorable as not only it provided lots of entertainment; it also increased our knowledge of how the film industry works. If Mekaal or I join this industry when we are older, there are so many avenues open for us outside acting. I think I may look into special effects when I am older, and a degree in computer science and artificial intelligence would come in handy for that.

We said goodbye to Universal Studios at 5 pm. Our next destination was the Hollywood Walk of Fame, but we were exhausted and wanted to get home before rush hour, so we passed on further activities for the day. Before we even reached the highway, Mekaal and I were fast asleep. It took us over two hours to get back to the hotel, and dad had to drag us out of the car. I remember only brushing my teeth and changing into PJs before tucking myself into bed.

The next morning, we woke up refreshed and decided to tour Long Beach and relax in the hotel. We had planned to visit Disney Land, but since we had already been to Euro Disney and others, it did not appeal to us anymore. That evening, we were invited to dinner by Beth Sanden, a friend of my dad's. Beth is a paraplegic athlete who holds multiple Guinness World Records. About 15 years ago, she had a bike accident when she was training for Ironman, which resulted in her getting paralysed from the waist down, only recovering enough to still need to walk with a stick. She uses a special handcycle to do her marathons and has been on almost all the trips dad has organised. We met at an Italian restaurant at Long Beach promenade and had a lovely evening with Beth and Burt.

Beth was incredibly nice and told us stories from her racing from around the world. Mekaal and I ordered tomato pasta while Dad had a steak. My pasta portion was huge, and I could only finish half the plate. At around 8 pm we said our goodbyes and drove back to the hotel. On the way, I did not feel too good as my stomach was hurting. Maybe I was run down from all the travelling, running, and sightseeing, so on our return it was lights out for us. In the middle of the night, I woke up feeling uneasy, and as I was about to get out of bed and rush to the bathroom, I threw up. It was not normal vomit; it continued one gush after another. It was so loud that dad woke up and turned the bedside table light on because he thought it was raining and water had somehow seeped in from the ceiling. But when we looked down, it was full of spaghetti and red sauce. It was everywhere - in my hair, on my clothes, on the bedsheet and the floor. We were all shell-shocked. I could not even talk at that point, and dad had to carry me to the bathroom where I threw up again inside and around the toilet bowl. The room was a total mess, and the stench was unbearable. Mekaal was asked to stay in bed and not move as dad found me some clean clothes. I had a quick shower, hoping not to puke in the tub too. As I came out of the bathroom, I saw the mess that I had created. There was no way dad could clean all that up. He opened the door so we could get some fresh air. Luckily, our bags had escaped the onslaught. Dad called mum in Doha. It was evening there, and he left a frantic voicemail for her to call us back. Mum called five minutes later as she was in a meeting, and dad put the conversation on speaker:

Dad: *"Zara just threw up all over the room. She's not well. The whole room is full of vomit, and it stinks. I don't know what to do."*

Mum: *"So, clean it up. What do you expect me to do? I am 12,000 miles away!"*

Dad: *"Oh, you have no idea how bad it is. No way, I can clean it up."*

Mum: *"Honey, I'm sorry, but I can't help you at all. Just change the room or ask the house staff to clean it."*

Dad: *"It's 2 am in LA!!! No house staff here. By the way, what should I give Zara to make her stop the vomiting?"*

Mum: *"Gosh, just give her Pepto-Bismol and she will be fine."*

Dad: *"We don't have that. Only painkillers. Never realised we would need that with us."*

Mum: *"It's OK, just drive to the pharmacy and buy it."*

All this time, mum was so cool while dad was running around like a headless chicken not knowing what to do. I spoke to mum, and she said I would be OK as long as I took the medicine, water, and a fizzy drink. She told me not to eat anything for another day. So, dad went to explain to reception and we were moved to another room. Poor Mekaal and dad had one eye on the skiddy floor and one on the scattered luggage as they carefully collected all the bags. With their noses covered, they quickly moved everything to the new room. I was given a bottle of cold water which I slowly sipped as I lay in bed. Mekaal was so nice that he put the garbage bin beside the bed, just in case. After settling us in, dad drove to a nearby pharmacy and returned with Pepto-Bismol and a Sprite which I took before returning to bed. Thankfully, there was nothing more to throw up as my stomach was empty, and I just needed to keep myself hydrated.

In the morning, dad went to our old room and the smell was so strong he had to leave immediately. A poor maid was busy inside cleaning up the mess, so he quietly handed her a twenty-dollar bill and apologised. This was our last day in LA, and our original plan was to drive up to Hollywood before heading to the airport. But given my delicate stomach, we decided not to spend so much time in the car or even walking around. At noon, we checked out of the hotel and made our way to LAX. The rest of the journey was smooth as we reached Doha after a long overnight flight. I took only juices and water for another day. Mum greeted us at arrivals. She gave me a big hug, and when we got home, she had a nice meal ready for us.

On the whole, the North American leg of the seven continents challenge was a blast. It started well with the marathon and sightseeing but ended up a little sour for me. I guess years down the road, we may forget the marathon, but the smell of tomato pasta puke will continue to haunt dad for a very long time!

CHAPTER 13

CONTINENT NO. 6
ASIA

NATIONAL SPORTS DAY ULTRA
Tuesday 13 February 2018
Education City, QATAR

Some of you may be wondering why this race took place on a Tuesday instead of the usual weekend. Before I get into a detailed analysis of the Asian leg of the challenge, let me explain the reason for this mid-week event. Back in 2012, the Emir of Qatar decided to announce the second Tuesday of February as a national holiday. The idea was to promote sports and educate the population on ways to reduce the health risks associated with a sedentary lifestyle. Illnesses like diabetes and heart disease are prevalent among the local population, along with childhood obesity. Along with health benefits, the holiday is also viewed as an opportunity to bring communities closer together through sports. Almost all companies in Qatar organise sports activities for their employees. Driving around Qatar on that day feels like we are watching the Olympics with the range of sporting activities including football, athletics, rowing, tennis, squash, martial arts, and many more. Mum is also really busy on Sports Day as she organises Playball classes at Qatar Foundation.

The previous November, Mekaal and I had a DNF during the race in Education City as we stopped after the half marathon mark, so this was our second attempt at clearing the hurdle. The race was organised by Qatar Ultra Runners, a group of trail running enthusiasts who launched the Qatar East-West Run a few years back. They wanted a 50 km event around Education City and were supported by Qatar Foundation to hold the race on their premises. Later, to attract more runners, they decided to allow different distances ranging from 7 to 50 km. Dad signed us up for it rather than us flying somewhere else in Asia to complete the challenge. It was not only a lot cheaper but also very convenient as the race starts no more than ten minutes from our home. It ticked all the boxes, and this time we were ready for the challenge. Runners planning to do the longer distance were encouraged to start early, while half marathoners started at 8 am together with a large contingent of walkers and cyclists. It was no ordinary race as the inauguration of the event was performed by HH Sheikha Moza bint Nasser, the Emir's mother. She is the most influential royal family member and the visionary behind the creation of Qatar Foundation and Education City - a huge 12 square kilometre campus serving eight top-class universities, state of the art sports facilities, a championship golf course and a stadium for the 2022 Football World Cup.

The race course was designed in a way that would take us past all the iconic structures of the complex. The start line was adjacent to *Ceremonial Court* overlooking the *Green Spine*. From there, runners made their way past the golf course toward Al Shaqab Horse Racing Academy and then around Carnegie Mellon and Weil Cornell campuses. The entire loop was a little over seven km which we needed to complete six times to finish the marathon. We were lucky to start the race early around dawn and managed to cover most of the distance before the sun started blazing down on the cobblestone streets of Education City. Runners who started the race at 8 am felt the burn, and many of them decided to downgrade the distance from anywhere between 7 and 21.1 km. For us, it was tough going after 9 am as there was no breeze and certainly no shade to protect us from the sun. Though the race took place in the relatively cooler month of February, running a full marathon, even at that time in the morning, is not easy. We were determined to complete the distance, though, as DNF was not an option anymore. Just when I was beginning to feel exhausted, I heard my name in the distance, and it was mum running towards us. She had been busy that day organising Playball classes but had decided to take a half-hour break to come and support us. She even brought us a doughnut and some Gatorade for instant energy. Her support helped a lot, and Mekaal and I were so pleased to see her. At around 10 am, Education City was buzzing as loads of families had arrived to take part in various other games. The atmosphere was electric with live bands, cheerleaders, and enthusiastic volunteers cheering the runners on. The organisers knew what we were planning to achieve, and hence, every time we completed a loop, they called our names over the microphone to show their full support. Loads of QRS runners were also part of the event, and we all knew each other. So after being on the course for over six hours, we made our final push and crossed the line together to complete continent number six! We made it, and it was extremely satisfying. There was one more surprise waiting for us as we crossed the finish line. I was first in the marathon, and Mekaal came third. The reason I was first was because other fast ladies could not take the heat and dropped off after a half marathon or at the 28 km mark.

Completion of continent number six

They were certainly faster than me, but I was the one who persevered and completed the race. Both Mekaal and I were called onto the podium to collect our big trophies.

So, there it was, a home marathon finally completed on the second try. We were both relieved that it did not involve another flight and another fight with time zones. It took us 10 minutes to get home, and we were ready to party that evening. When mum got back, we went out to my favourite restaurant, PF Chang, for a lovely meal. One more continent to go, and we were ready, but we had to wait another month.

CHAPTER 14

Continent No. 7
Oceania

CBR.48HR
Friday 16 March 2018
Canberra, ACT, AUSTRALIA

A month after our last race in Qatar, we were ready for the finale down under. We were both busy with school and after-school commitments, so our cardiovascular levels were in top shape. We were running local races, including triathlons, and Mekaal was preoccupied with football matches. A week before we were scheduled to fly out, Mekaal's school team had reached the inter-school football final. Being a key member of the team, the coach wanted him to play. This made dad extremely nervous, as any injury a day before we flew to Australia would have been disastrous. Mum spoke with the coach and advised him to let Mekaal play only if needed. However, there was no stopping Mekaal as he wanted his team to lift the trophy. It seems the football final was more important to him than us breaking the world record. As luck would have it, his team won the final, and he did not get injured. Dad must have breathed a sigh of relief when he received the news.

On Thursday, 15 March 2018, we left for Hamad International Airport one last time on our marathon quest. Yet again we were on a morning flight leaving at 7 am, so mum dropped us off a few hours before. It was Qatar Airways direct to Sydney covering a distance of 12,400 km over the Indian Ocean and mainland Australia for over 14 hours. As it was a day flight, we had nothing better to do than watch inflight entertainment again. By then, I had pretty much watched every decent movie on the plane, so there was nothing new. Nonetheless, I kept myself occupied by reading a novel by Cynthia Kadohata called *Kira Kira,* which was about a Japanese-American family who lived in Iowa in the 1950s. Other than reading, nothing much changed. It was the same meal menu, followed by unlimited helpings of juices, crisps, and ice cream. I sat in the aisle so as not to bug Mekaal and dad when I had to use the washroom. We flew over mainland Australia in complete darkness and finally landed at Sydney Airport on the Friday morning. Our journey wasn't over yet as our destination was Canberra. Dad had booked this flight in November, and a month later, Qatar Airways had launched a new service to Canberra. So, the same plane that we arrived in Sydney on was going to fly to Canberra after an hour. Unfortunately, we couldn't change the ticket; dad even tried upon arriving in Sydney, but they refused. So, instead of a half an hour flight, we had to take a four-hour bus to Canberra, which we had pre-booked. So, there we were, in a packed bus heading to the nation's capital after a 14-hour flight. Both Mekaal and I were exhausted, and we slept part of the way. On arrival, we took a taxi to the AIS Athletics Track, which was a good 20-minute drive away. The cab driver didn't know where the track was, so he dropped us off at the entrance of the main stadium. After asking around, we were shown the direction and had to walk for another ten minutes to get to the race start.

The event was a little different from most marathons. Much like South Africa, it was a multi-day event with various distances, only this time, it was to be run on a 400m outdoor track. We met the race director, Billy Pearce, who was so nice even to allow us to take part. Dad found Australian race directors the most rigid of all people to communicate with. He contacted probably ten or 12 organisers, but they all refused us based on our age. Billy was the only one to allow us as he said his ten-year-old son had run a marathon, so he was extremely sympathetic towards us. The marathon event started at 5 pm, so we had four hours to kill. Dad had booked a tent for us to sleep in, just like South Africa, but due to some logistical hiccup, the tent never arrived. We were exhausted and sleep-deprived, but there was nowhere to rest. After waiting around for a couple of hours, dad booked us a room at a nearby RV Park with bungalow type accommodation. We had a whole clean, spacious two-bedroom bungalow to ourselves. But there wasn't much time to rest as the race start was in a few hours. We ordered a cab which didn't show up, and after waiting more than half an hour, panic started setting in. We just couldn't miss the start of the race, so dad went out to the main road and hailed a cab which brought us to the start line 15 minutes before the gun went off.

So there we were, at the start line for the final race of the seven continents challenge. Exhausted after over 24 hours of commuting on planes, busses and taxis, we were about to create history. Between us and the record was a mere 100+ loops of a 400m track, on no sleep. We didn't care as our adrenaline was high and we just wanted it all to finish. Mekaal set off at a blistering pace, and within 23 minutes, we had completed 5 km. I stayed back with dad and maintained a steady pace, while Mekaal went on to lap us a few times until dad asked him to slow down or he would burn himself out. As usual, he didn't listen, and as predicted by 10 km, he was walking. With all the circling around, my left calf felt extremely tight, and I was in a lot of pain. Dad quickly took out some painkillers from the bag and made me drink the syrup. Then he suddenly noticed a massage therapist, so on the next loop, he walked me to her. She was an American lady and decided to treat me on the spot. After 10 minutes of poking and prodding, I was ready to hit the round and round circus again. By that time, Mekaal was already about five loops ahead of me. Later, dad felt the same pain and decided to get a massage too. I think he just wanted an excuse as he is a massage junkie so would jump at any available opportunity.

To avoid injuries due to repetitive movement around the short track, the race organisers allowed runners to change direction every two hours. When dad had been on the Guinness World Record trail for the seven continents ultra, he had run a 50 km race on a 400 m track in Melbourne. He didn't mind that race and told us that we would soon get used to running around. But I found it painful, and Mekaal was already walking most of the race. The only thing in our favour was the weather. Since we were running at night, there was a nice cool breeze and no hot sun to worry about. So, we ran and ran and ran around in circles and kept checking the monitor beside the finish line. Every time we crossed the 400m line, it would show the number of loops and the distance we had covered. I was behind dad and Mekaal, but I didn't mind. Finally, after seven hours on that dreaded track, Mekaal was the first one to cross the finish line to complete the race, followed by dad a few minutes later. I still had three more laps to run, and on the final one, Mekaal joined me while dad had the camera ready for the finish. Billy Pearce, the RD of the event, was standing beside the finish line and he took the microphone and started the commentary. Our last 100 metres was a full out dash, and as we crossed the finish line, we heard:

Billy: *"So here are Zara and Mekaal crossing the finish line to complete the marathon. They have become the youngest female and male to complete a marathon on all seven continents. How do you feel Zara and Mekaal?"*

Me: *"Amazing!"*

Mekaal: *"Oh, I am so tired."*

Billy: *"How do you feel proud dad?"*

Dad: *"I am so proud of the kids. They were unbelievable."*

With RD Billy Pearce after breaking the world record

We got our customary finish line kiss from dad and gathered for photos. Mekaal and I had achieved what we set out to do, and at the end, we were standing erect. We had proved all the doubters wrong. No injuries were sustained in the seven races around the world, and we were proud of our achievements. Over nine months we had spent almost 200 hours on planes, buses, and cars covering a distance of over 110,000 km. At age 11, I was a new World Record holder for the youngest female to complete a marathon on all seven continents, and Mekaal had achieved the same in the male category at the tender age of 10. Together, we had shattered six official World Records, which was subsequently confirmed by the records body a few weeks after we submitted our claims. Next day, we slept till 2 pm then left for Sydney to do some sightseeing before returning to Qatar. Mum met us at the airport with a big sign marking our achievement. The celebrations went on for weeks with press coverage in Qatar, the UK, and even in Canada. We were featured in top newspapers and magazines around the world.

However, for us, the important thing was the bet. A few days after arriving in Doha, dad took us to the mall and bought Mekaal a PS4, and I got my first smartphone. Now, I look back and wonder if it was all worth it. My 12th birthday was a month away, and I could have asked him for a phone for that, but I knew that was too easy. The seven continents adventure taught us real life lessons, not least being no matter how tough the situation is, if we put our minds to something, we will achieve our goals. I feel that in those nine months of travelling and running around the world, we gained more knowledge and confidence than any school books could have taught us in five years. Mekaal and I can only thank our parents for this as they are the ones who had the vision and trust in us to achieve our goals. I am sure both of us will remember that in the years to come when we face any hurdles in our lives. If ordinary kids like us can achieve those goals, everyone can.

A few months after we broke the records, another conversation started at the dinner table:

Dad: *"So guys, how about another challenge?"*

Me: *"No, absolutely no more challenges."*

Dad: *'C'mon, you would love the new one!"*

Mekaal: *"What is it, dad?"*

Dad: *"Let's do the Three Peaks Challenge. Climb the highest points in Scotland, England, and Wales."*

Me: *"No way. I am not doing it."*

Mekaal: *"If I do it, will you buy me a smartphone?"*

Dad: *"Of course, deal!"*

Mekaal: *"C'mon Zara, let's do it!"*

Me: *"OK, fine, but I want a new iPhone!"*

Dad: *"Dammit, OK, deal!"*

CHAPTER 15

OFFICIAL WORLD RECORDS

ZARA RAHIM

The youngest person to complete a marathon on each continent (Female) is 11 Years, 9 Months and 16 Days.

The youngest person to complete an ultramarathon in Antarctica (Female) is 11 Years, 6 Months and 16 Days.

The youngest siblings to complete a marathon on each continent is 21 Years, 11 Months and 22 Days.

The youngest siblings to complete an ultramarathon in Antarctica is 21 Years, 5 Months and 22 Days.

MEKAAL RAHIM

The youngest person to complete a marathon on each continent (Male) is 10 Years, 2 Months and 6 Days.

The youngest person to complete an ultramarathon in Antarctica (Male) is 9 Years, 11 Months and 6 Days.

The youngest siblings to complete a marathon on each continent is 21 Years, 11 Months and 22 Days.

The youngest siblings to complete an ultramarathon in Antarctica is 21 Years, 5 Months and 22 Days.

SEVEN CONTINENTS FUN FACTS

TRAVELLING TIME & DISTANCE COVERED

Total distance covered: 111,096 km

Total flying & transit time: 171 hours

CHAPTER 16

3 PEAKS CHALLENGE

SCOTLAND – ENGLAND – WALES
13 to 15 August 2019

I had my first taste of mountains back in 2011 when we had a family holiday in Nepal. Dad was taking part in the Annapurna 100 while mum decided to trek the range to kill time. She hired two Sherpas to carry us up the steep climb. In the end, we preferred to walk, but from what I remember, it was quite tiring. After all, I was four years old, and Mekaal was about to turn three. After that, we regularly visited the northern areas of Pakistan over the next many years for marathons and sightseeing. However, we didn't do any serious climbing apart from walking up some old forts and historical landmarks.

In the summer of 2018, we had our first real experience of climbing when dad took us to Ben Lomond, considered the ninth easiest of the 282 climbable Munros. A Munro is any mountain in Scotland over 3,000 feet high. As most of them start at sea-level, bagging a Munro involves a lot of climbing over a short distance, so one needs to be fit. We made our way up to the summit with quite a bit of moaning and complaining, but on the way down we forgot all the hardships. The breath-taking views are a sight to behold.

A year later, we were ready to take on a bigger challenge; this time, the reward was to be a smartphone for each of us. For me, it was an upgrade while Mekaal was going to get his first smartphone at age 11. Dad was busy organising the Southern African Challenge, and since it was Eid holidays in Qatar, he flew from Johannesburg to Edinburgh to spend a week with us and do the challenge. I must say, though we were excited to get new phones, neither Mekaal nor I were too keen on climbing. Maybe it was a fear of heights or the prospect of climbing many peaks in a short time, but chickening out was not an option. As dad landed in Edinburgh, he asked mum to take him to the mountaineering store immediately to pick up all the essentials. I have no idea where he gets all his energy from. He had organised and run seven marathons in seven countries in a week in Africa, including all the travelling in between races, and then took a long overnight flight to Scotland. Somehow, after all that, he still had enough energy to take us on a climbing expedition. I guess this is how he likes to spend his holidays rather than lying around on a beach in an all-you-can-eat resort.

After careful planning, we were ready to embark on this new adventure. Due to mum's lederhosen disease, dad suggested she shouldn't climb but instead be our official driver. That was a tough job as the distances between the three peaks involved long hours of driving, mainly on small country roads. We decided to tackle Ben Nevis first. At 4,413 feet above sea level, it is the highest peak in the UK. We started with Ben Nevis because we wanted fresh legs and also, it was closer to home. So, we set out from Glasgow just after 8 am and drove 175 km to Fort William. The journey via the A82 took close to three and a half hours. It was almost lunchtime when we got there, and we grabbed a quick sandwich and took the scenic route up. The plan was to take a maximum of two breaks en route to the summit, and one on the way down so that we would be finished within seven or eight hours.

We climbed steadily as we followed the clearly laid out path featuring rocky stairs and gravel. It was wide enough in most places to accommodate oncoming trekkers. We had walking sticks and a backpack containing extra gloves, hoodies, waterproofs and some food and drink.

Dad carried most of the bulky stuff, especially bottles of Irn-Bru and water. On the way up, dad gave us regular data updates as his Garmin watch displayed the distance, time, and height. At one particular spot, an elderly couple started a conversation with us as they had overheard dad mentioning the height. The wife was so pleased to hear that we had climb 600m since we started.

She said had it not been for us, she would have walked down thinking we were so far away from the top. Dad asked them to tag along with us so that they could hear his regular broadcasts, and they happily obliged, staying close to us.

At around 800m up, we noticed two different tracks. The left one was clear but long and loopy, while the right one was not marked but was leading to the top. To save time, we opted for the tough, steeper one, which turned out to be a disaster. It was boggy, and we all got our feet wet; in the end, it probably took us longer. Oh well, that was an adventure, but not one to be repeated any time soon. At around 1,000 m, I was beginning to feel cold and tired, so we stopped for a while to eat a sandwich and enjoy the beautiful views. It was a clear day, but there were clouds above so we could not see the peak. We continued our ascent as the path became steadily tougher with rocks and pebbles replacing the finely manicured paths further down. Ben Nevis is deceptive in that you think you have almost reached the top as you can't see up ahead, but there are false summits, and we still needed to go up and up. We finally made it to the top in very little visibility. Then suddenly it dawned on me that I was standing at the highest point in the UK.

Highest point in UK – Ben Nevis summit

That was cool, yet very cold and windy so after five minutes we started our descent. The views coming down were spectacular, more so because we were descending so we could enjoy them more. So, after a little over seven hours, we were back, and mum was waiting for us with a Ben Nevis completion medal, a certificate, and *"I conquered Ben Nevis"* T-shirts. One peak was conquered, and it was time to start the four-hour drive back to Glasgow. We reached home around midnight and got ready for bed as the next day would be another long drive and tough climb for us.

We set out south on the A74 for a 250 km journey to Scafell Pike in the Lake District National Park. Standing at 978m or 3,209 feet high, it is the highest mountain in England. It was a good 1,200 feet lower than Ben Nevis, which we climbed the day before, so we were quite confident in our abilities to scale this height. The weather was atrocious on the journey. The rain was relentless on the motorway and did not stop all the way to the Lake District. Once we exited the motorway, we had to drive through small winding roads and did not see a single sign for the mountain. This was strange as we had expected some sort of signage to the highest mountain in England. Perhaps the English weren't too proud of their highest peak as it pales in comparison to the ones in Scotland and Wales. If it weren't for SATNAV, we wouldn't have been able to find the place. As the GPS narrowed in towards our destination, we reluctantly entered the gates of a camping ground hoping we were in the right place. There was an office on the left from where a friendly gentleman emerged. Dad asked him if we were in the right place, and he nodded and showed us the path to go up. We were all in shock realising that there wasn't even a gift shop from which to buy souvenirs. We would have happily bought a fridge magnet or a T-shirt had there been something on display. Anyway, we were ready to go after a quick dash to the stinky, filthy washroom. We were also lucky with the weather as right about when we set off, the rain stopped. On the way up, we met a trekker coming back and asked him how the conditions were at the top. He told us that he decided to quit the ascent as he was expecting the weather to get really bad and the climb dangerous. We stood there and thought for a while and then decided to gamble. Dad insisted we continue with the climb and in case the weather turns bad, we can always return. Getting to the main path required us to cross a couple of bridges bringing us to a narrow path beside a stream. The hurdle came when we had to cross the stream, which meant navigating through boulders and fast-flowing, knee-deep water. We weren't prepared for this, and it took us a while to find our way. I was, as usual, the slowest and dad and Mekaal had to wait.

"C'mon slowcoach, we don't have all day," shouted Mekaal as he stood waiting for me on the other side of the stream.
"Quiet Mekaal, I don't want to hurt myself. I'm coming!" I screamed at him while still deciding which path to take.

By the time I crossed, my feet were drenched, and I needed a change of socks to continue. From there on, it was a climb up rocky steps as far as we could see. We knew the mountain top was further up, but due to fog, we could not see ahead. It was a relatively easy climb though, and in the distance, we saw beautiful lakes all around the mountain. After we passed 700m, the steepness flattened out a bit, but the path became rocky. We were under the clouds with very little visibility. Unlike Ben Nevis, there were hardly any other climbers, so a few times we got a little lost. Then, in the distance, we heard music, which was odd. A group of South Asians were walking up with their friends, and we decided to follow them to the top. It was one last push up the stacked-up boulders leading to the summit at 978m. Yes, we made it and were standing on the highest place in England with our arms aloft for the perfect photo.

Since it was all foggy, there was no point hanging around. Halfway down Mekaal crossed paths with some mountain sheep and decided to run after them. He still gets a thrill from doing silly things. I, on the other hand, sat on a big stone eating a sandwich with dad while enjoying the beautiful vistas.

Getting down was a little tricky as the man-made steps which we took coming up turned out to be very slippery on the way down. I was extremely cautious on those stairs as one slip could have resulted in a sprained ankle or more serious injury. Although Mekaal and dad were well ahead, I didn't care and took my time coming down. There was one last hurdle to overcome, that dreaded crossing of the stream. By the time we got there, the stream was flowing much faster than before, and it took me 25 minutes to cross it. It was dangerous and slippery, but only Mekaal had the guts to jump quickly from one boulder to another. Dad and I were more cautious, but we made it through. Mum was waiting for us in the car park as we arrived back. She had been on her own little adventure driving through some small roads in the

Lake District. We quickly changed our climbing gear and settled into something more comfortable as we had another five-hour drive to our hotel in Wales. Mekaal and I slept in the car while mum and dad talked and listened to an audiobook all the way to our hotel in Chester.

Next morning, we woke up with stiff legs and decided to chill in the hotel. We were exhausted, and mum also needed some rest with all the driving she had done. Our destination was less than two hours away, and the weather was expected to be sunny for the climb in the afternoon. It all worked out well for us as when we arrived at the base of Snowdon, there was bright sunshine. Unlike Scafell Pike, Snowdon National Park was buzzing with activity. The promenade was full of souvenir shops, restaurants, and bars. There was even a steam train that takes tourists to the top. Mekaal sheepishly asked dad if we could take that up and then walk down, but the answer was a stern no. Away from all the hustle and bustle, we followed the tourist path towards the mountain. It was wide and very well marked.

We could see where we were heading for miles, and there were plenty of trekkers on the way. Mum would have loved this kind of trek as the underfoot conditions were extremely good. Every five minutes or so, we would see the steam train carrying visitors up and down the mountain. However, we preferred the climb as we got to experience so much along the way. It took us about three hours to get to the top with only one stop en route. The summit was jam-packed with tourists, mostly the ones who had arrived by train. However, we managed to climb up and find a spot to take our summit photo. Afterwards, we wanted hot chocolate, but the queues were long. It wasn't worth it, so we decided to head back.

On the way back, we had our usual fun and banter. Dad, as usual, was coming up with other adventures, and I was saying no before he even finished the sentence. We descended the mountain in two hours and walked straight into a restaurant for ice cream. Mum wasn't expecting us back that early, so she was out getting steak pies - dad's favourite - and turkey sandwiches for us. We were thrilled to have completed the challenge. It wasn't as tough as we had expected, but then again, we were comparing it with running seven marathons on seven continents.

Shortly afterwards, we began heading back to Glasgow, and my poor mum had to drive us again. So, in three days, we climbed

10,052 feet over a 37 km trek. The total distance travelled was approximately 1,600 km which took around 22 hours of driving along small roads in poor weather. If anyone deserved a medal and recognition for this challenge, it would have to be mum. We all congratulated ourselves on the return journey and reached Glasgow around midnight.

The 3 Peaks Challenge was done and dusted, and now it was time to drag daddy to the shops to collect our prizes. But that had to wait till we reached Doha. I really wonder why dad always falls into this trap. It surely won't be the last, as soon he would no doubt start bugging us to join him on another crazy adventure.

CHAPTER 17

LOVE HATE RELATIONSHIP WITH KARATE

Proud to receive my black belt after 7 years of hard work

Disney has been entertaining kids around the world for generations. They started with the theme parks followed by movies, cartoons, cruises, and even their own TV channels. So, like everyone else, I was glued to Disney from a young age. As you grow older, Disney introduces age-appropriate channels. Apparently, their programs are streamed through 46 channels in 33 languages. So, from watching Disney Junior as a young kid to Disney XD as I grew older, I was hooked on some programs that I would watch every day. One such show that I fell in love with was *Kickin' It,* a martial arts-based comedy program based on a karate school which had the reputation of being the worst dojo in the Bobby Wasabi chain of schools. So, the company hires a new instructor to improve the image of the school. I found the show quite funny and was mesmerised by the karate skills taught to the students. I wanted to learn martial arts and be able to kick, punch and break bricks with my bare hands.

I asked mum and dad if they could find a karate school for me. Mekaal quickly joined in the conversation and wanted to sign up too. Finding a school wasn't hard at all as there was a karate academy five minutes' drive from our house. The timings were perfect, three times a week from 5 to 7 pm. We were hooked, and for the first year or two, I walked, talked and breathed karate. Whether it was kata or kumite, I excelled in both and passed all my exams in the first try. By the time we got to blue belt, we had to move to another karate academy which was a good 45 minutes' drive away in rush hour traffic. Mekaal had lost interest by then, so I quit with him. It just did not interest me anymore, as my passion had moved from karate to music and acting.

For two years, I stayed away from karate, but I knew dad wasn't happy about it. He saw the potential in me and encouraged me to complete the task I had started. He said it's a life lesson never to give up, as he had quit karate as a yellow belt. So, after I completed the marathon world record, I decided to re-enrol in the program and work towards the black belt. However, it was the same issue again with long commutes and long waits for the exam. Eventually, dad found another karate institute and took me for an interview. The sensei was very impressed with my technique and worked with me for almost a year and a half. During that time, I was able to pass all three brown belt exams. The final exam for the black belt was scheduled for April 2020, but then coronavirus put the whole world in a freeze and all classes were cancelled. However, the sensei decided to conduct the classes via Zoom, and I completed three months of training from the comfort of my living room. I passed the black belt exam right after my 14th birthday. It was a huge relief that a journey that had started as an obsession seven years earlier was finally completed through sheer hard work and many hours of practice. Looking back, I am glad I finished it. I know this is what dad wanted. He didn't want me to give up as he was worried that I might develop a habit of quitting.

Receiving the black belt certificate from Sensei Najmal Ibrahim

Obtaining a black belt in karate was more of a life lesson than an accomplishment. He said that when I grow up and enter university or professional life, there will be times when I have my back against the wall, and the odds will be stacked against me. When that happens, only people with a strong will and relentless attitude end up overcoming the odds and finding a way to defeat any resistance.

My journeys around the world, breaking records and completing challenging tasks that I didn't enjoy, has indeed taught me vital life lessons. I have also realised that I need to follow my passion rather than be told what I should do when I grow up. Over dinner, Mekaal and I usually have long conversations with our parents about what we should study in university and what professions we should pursue. They also share their experiences and knowledge but also advise us that in the end, it's up to us what paths we carve out for ourselves. My brother and I are still young, so we have a long time to think about our futures. However, one thing is for sure; I will always consult my family every step of the way as I know they will always look out for my best interests.

The journey continues…..

- THE END -

ABOUT THE AUTHORS

Zara Rahim is a long-distance runner, martial arts expert, triathlete, and an accomplished swimmer. In 2018, at just 11 years of age, she set a world record for being the youngest female to complete a full marathon on all seven continents. She also became the youngest female to complete an ultra-marathon (50 km) in Antarctica when she crossed the finish line on King George Island in December 2017.

Zara holds four official world records in long-distance running. Zara and her brother, Mekaal, broke the world record for the youngest siblings to complete a marathon on each continent, and the youngest siblings to complete an ultra-marathon in Antarctica. She has run more than 100 long-distance races in over 20 countries, including over 40 podium finishes in her category.

In 2020, she was awarded a black belt in Shotokan karate. She is fluent in English and French. Her other hobbies include drama, photography, music, and travel. To-date, Zara has visited over 65 countries and of course, thanks to her world records, has covered all seven continents.

Ziyad Rahim is a banker by profession, and a keen sports enthusiast. He holds ten Guinness World Records in long-distance running. In 2015, he became the first athlete in the world to complete an ultra-marathon, full marathon, and half marathon on each continent. Ziyad is a member of the seven continents marathon club, having completed the circuit seven times. To-date, Ziyad has completed over 200 long-distance races in 70+ countries.

In November 2015, Ziyad started Z Adventures (www.z-adventures.org), a marathon travel company specialising in bespoke running adventures around the world. The company organises marathons in over 40 countries across six continents; more than any other adventure-travel company in the world. Their flagship adventures include cruise marathon vacations in the Caribbean, the highest road marathon in the world in Northern Pakistan (as approved by Guinness World Records), a unique running adventure in the secluded island of Socotra, Yemen; and various other multi-country running challenges in Asia, Europe, South America, Antarctica and Africa.

Printed in Great Britain
by Amazon